between

a journey through Proverbs

God & me

between

a journey through Proverbs

God & me

BY
VICKI COURTNEY

B&H
PUBLISHING GROUP

between God & me:

a journey through proverbs

ISBN: 978-0-8054-4985-3

Dewey Decimal Classification: 248.82

Subject Heading: CHRISTIAN LIFE \ BIBLE. O.T. PROVERBS—STUDY \ GIRLS

2 3 4 5 6 7 8 9 10   14 13 12 11 10

Check this out!

Author's Web Sites

VickiCourtney.com: stay up to date with the latest information regarding Vicki's books, speaking engagements, or invite her to speak at your event.

Virtuousreality.com: an online magazine for middle and high school girls highlighting relevant articles, a blog feature, a prayer board, and artist of the month.

VirtueAlert.com: Vicki's blog geared to parents highlighting issues relevant in today's culture.

Other books by Vicki Courtney from B&H:

Between: A Girl's Guide to Life

Between Us Girls: Fun Talk about Faith, Friends, & Family

5 Conversations You Must Have with Your Daughter

Your Girl: Raising a Godly Daughter in an Ungodly World

Yada Yada: A Devotional Journal for Moms

More Than Just Talk: A Journal for Girls

The Virtuous Woman: Shattering the Superwoman Myth

TeenVirtue: Real Issues, Real Life . . . A Teen Girl's Survival Guide

TeenVirtue 2: A Teen Girl's Guide to Relationships

TeenVirtue Confidential: Your Questions About God, Guys, and Getting Older

Your Boy: Raising a Godly Son in an Ungodly World

Contents

JUST BETWEEN US

Proverbs 1-5

Proverbs 6-10

Proverbs 11-15

Proverbs 16-20

Proverbs 21-25

Proverbs 26-31

About the Author:

Vicki Courtney is a best-selling author, speaker, and the creator of virtuousreality.com, an online magazine for teen girls. She lives in Austin, Texas, with her husband, Keith and their three children, Ryan, Hayden, and Paige. In her spare time she enjoys running, shopping, and spending time with her family.

Favorite grade in school: 5th

Least favorite grade in school: 11th (Blah!)

Biggest pet peeve: People who talk on their cell phones in public restrooms!

Favorite restaurant food: Tex-Mex (If you're from Texas, you'll know what it is!)

Sports played growing up: Gymnastics, track, cheerleading (yes, it's a sport!)

Funny memory: In 4th grade I begged my mom for a pair of tennis shoes that all my friends had and when I finally got them, I slept in them the first night!

Not-so-funny memory: My 6th grade teacher took up a note I was passing to a friend and read it out loud to the class! (More about that in this book!)

Susan Jones wrote all the quizzes and interactive pieces in this issue of *Between*. She is a former event director and has worked for both Virtuous Reality Ministries and Prestonwood Christian Academy. She has contributed to the *Between* and *TeenVirtue* series by Vicki Courtney. Currently she is pursuing full-time missions in Guatemala. You can follow her journey at www.susankayjones.wordpress.com.

Favorite Friday night activity: Pizza and a rented movie

Biggest pet peeve: When people scrape food off their fork with their teeth! I can't stand that sound!

Sports played growing up: Dance, gymnastics, cheerleading, and softball

Countries visited on mission trips: Guatemala, Peru, Nicaragua, and Dominican Republic

Weird birthday gift request: Cute office supplies. They just make me happy!

Favorite candy: Junior Mints or York Peppermint Patties for movies, and Peanut M&Ms for everything else

Favorite books of the Bible: 1 Corinthians, Romans, and 1 Peter

LIFE is all about choices. Sometimes we will make good choices and sometimes we will make bad choices. At your age, you may face simple choices like what flavor of ice cream to order at your favorite ice cream hangout, what color to paint your bedroom, or whether or not to trip your sister the next time she walks through the room after she tapes over your favorite TV show. (The answer is no!) You may also face more difficult choices like whether or not to watch a movie at your friend's house that wouldn't meet your parents' approval or whether or not you should let your best friend copy your homework before school starts. (No, again!) Some of you have faced really big choices like whether or not to go to private school or public school or which parent you should live with after your parents get a divorce. (Sorry, can't help you on those two!)

I wish I could tell you that as you get older, the choices you face will get easier. The truth is, they will get harder and harder. No one is perfect, so it makes sense that we could all use a little help when it comes to making as many wise choices as possible while we're here in this great big world. That's what I love about a book in the Bible called "Proverbs." It is full of advice on how to make the kind of choices that lead to a long and happy life. Most important, it offers us a road map to making the kind of choices that would honor God and make Him smile. In fact, read for yourselves what it says in the very first Proverb:

The purpose of these proverbs is to teach people wisdom and discipline, and to help them understand wise sayings. Through these proverbs, people will receive instruction in discipline, good conduct, and doing what is right, just, and fair. These proverbs will make the simpleminded clever. They will give knowledge and purpose to young people. Let those who are wise listen to these proverbs and become even wiser. And let those who understand receive guidance by exploring the depth of meaning in these proverbs, parables, wise sayings, and riddles. (Proverbs 1:2–6 NLT)

In this issue of *Between*, we're going to do just that: explore the depth of meaning in the proverbs. There is an article for each of the thirty-one proverbs and at the end of each article, I included a few questions to help you apply the proverb to your own life. The cool thing about this book is that you can read through it alone, go through it with your mom or dad, or use it in a Bible study with a group of friends. By the end of the book, my prayer is that you'll be as wise as an owl when it comes to making good and godly choices in life. And "hoo" wouldn't want that? (Sorry, I just couldn't resist!)

–Vicki Courtney

Proverbs 1-5

Proverbs 1

Proverbs 1:10 My child, if sinners entice you, turn your back on them!

Proverbs 1:15 Don't go along with them, my child! Stay far away from their paths.

When I was in 5th grade, I had one of those moments verse 10 talks about where I was "enticed by sinners" and I failed to "turn my back on them." I was invited to spend the night at a girl's house from my school named Christy. I had never been to her house before, so needless to say, I was pretty excited about the invitation. She also invited another girl from our class named Julie. Our friendship began one afternoon when our teacher awarded us some free time at the end of the day. She handed out Tootsie Roll Pops to the entire class after we all made A's on a spelling quiz. Now, what you probably don't know is that back when I was in 5th grade, there was this commercial on TV about Tootsie Roll Pops and the slogan was "How many licks does it take to get to the center of a Tootsie Roll Pop?" So yeah, this goofy guy in our class pretty much challenged the entire class to see "how many licks it would take to get to the center of our Tootsie Roll Pop" during our free time. I'm not sure why the teacher went along with the crazy challenge, but she did.

So, for the next hour, we licked and counted, licked and counted, determined to solve the mystery. By the time the bell rang, everyone had given up on the challenge and chewed their way to the gooey center, except for me, Julie, and Christy. Our tongues were bright red and for some reason that was awfully funny to our classmates, and they were cracking up at us while packing up their backpacks to head out the door. I don't really remember who won the challenge or, for that matter, how many licks it took to get to the center, but I do know the Tootsie Roll Pop challenge forged our friendship that day. From that day forward, we saved each other a spot at the lunch table and passed notes back and forth in class.

We were friends for a couple of months when the invitation to spend the night at Christy's house came. My mom dropped me off on that Friday night after meeting Christy's mom and then left. But there was a problem. Shortly after I got there, Christy's mom also left and said she probably wouldn't be back until the next morning. I had never stayed in my own house alone at night, much less someone else's! When I asked Christy where her mom was going, she said she was going to her "boyfriend's house to spend the night" and just kind of shrugged it off like it was no big deal. It was clear this wasn't the first time Christy had been left alone for the night before.

Julie showed up after Christy's mom left and her mom didn't even come to the door, so she didn't know there wasn't a grown up there. I remember thinking I should call my mom, but so many things were going through my head. I knew that if I called my mom to come and get me, Christy and Julie might think I was a scaredy-cat or call me a "baby." They both seemed really comfortable staying alone and it was then I realized the Christy and Julie I knew from school had a totally different home life than I did. Both of them lived with their moms and had very little supervision. They were allowed to do just about anything they wanted to do and were accustomed to staying home alone, sometimes even overnight.

A couple of hours after I got there, I experienced a Proverbs 1:10 moment where I was "enticed by sin." Christy got a lighter and suggested we light the cigarette butts her mom left in an ashtray to see what smoking was like.

I'm ashamed to say I gave into peer pressure and gave it a try. After choking and coughing until I thought I might die, I came to my senses and called my mom and told her to come and get me. I knew I was in over my head and these girls were moving much too fast for me. I told them I didn't feel good, which after my coughing attack and the nausea I felt from inhaling the cigarette smoke, was at least partially true.

After that night, things began to cool down in our friendship. I realized they were headed down a path I wasn't comfortable with and it was time to find a new group of friends. Sadly, years later, I heard they both struggled with using drugs and I was so thankful I chose to "stay far from their path."

Have you ever been "enticed by sin"?

JUST BETWEEN US

1. Write down Proverbs 1:10 just as it is in your Bible:

2. How was I "enticed by sinners" in the story above? (enticed = tempted)

3. Can you think of a time when you were "enticed by sin"? What happened?

4. Did you "go along" with those who enticed you or did you "stay far from their paths" (see Proverbs 1:15)?

5. It's important to remember that we are all "sinners." Can you think of a time when you "enticed" someone to do something wrong?

PSSST, GOD!

Take a minute to talk to God and ask Him to give you the strength to turn your back when others entice you to sin. Ask Him to forgive you for times when you were the one who enticed others to sin.

Say WHAT?

Understanding some of the strange sayings of Proverbs

"Let the wise listen and add to their learning, and let the discerning get guidance—for understanding proverbs and parables, the sayings and riddles of the wise." (Proverbs 1:5–6 NIV)

"Say What?" is designed to help you understand some of those weird, not-so-normal phrases you will read in this journey through Proverbs. Jesus spoke in parables (stories) to help illustrate or explain a truth He was trying to teach, but sometimes the disciples (you know, those twelve guys who hung out with Him all the time?) had to ask Him to explain it to them. So don't feel bad if you don't understand something you read. Ask your mom, dad, or a Sunday school teacher to help you out when you run across one of those "Say what?" moments!

Honor the LORD with your wealth, with the firstfruits of all your crops; then your barns will be filled to overflowing, and your vats will brim over with new wine."
(Proverbs 3:9–10 NIV)

In Bible times people would offer the first portion (part) of their crops to the temple where they worshipped God. "Firstfruits" helped support or take care of the religious leaders who worked in the temple. Maybe you've heard of the word *tithe*, which means to pay or give a tenth of something (like your money), typically to the church. Some of you may even tithe your allowance, which is great!

In this Proverb we are encouraged to honor God with what He has given us by offering some of it back to Him. Maybe you're thinking, "No way, that's my money," but the truth is, it all belongs to God. The second part of the verse reminds us that God will take care of us if we are obedient to Him.

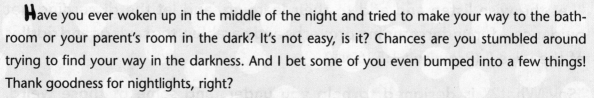

The path of the righteous is like the first gleam of dawn, shining ever brighter till the full light of day. But the way of the wicked is like deep darkness; they do not know what makes them stumble.
(Proverbs 4:18-19 NIV)

Have you ever woken up in the middle of the night and tried to make your way to the bathroom or your parent's room in the dark? It's not easy, is it? Chances are you stumbled around trying to find your way in the darkness. And I bet some of you even bumped into a few things! Thank goodness for nightlights, right?

The verse above tells us the way of the wicked is kind of like stumbling around in the dark . . . but all the time! Thankfully Jesus came to bring light to the world. If you are a Christian, then you have the light of Jesus inside you. The Bible also says He has given us His Word through the Bible and it is a "lamp to my feet." This means it teaches us how to live without stumbling or getting hurt because of sin. Jesus says those who live like this are like a city on a hill . . . our light cannot be hidden! Like a city on a hill, you can see the light from far, far away! The more we mature as Christians, the brighter our light gets! Kind of makes me want to sing that familiar song most of us grew up singing in church: "This little light of mine . . . I'm gonna to let it shine." Yeah, I know—it's stuck in your head now, isn't it?

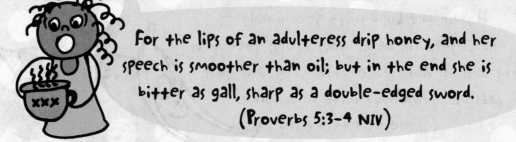

For the lips of an adulteress drip honey, and her speech is smoother than oil; but in the end she is bitter as gall, sharp as a double-edged sword.
(Proverbs 5:3-4 NIV)

In this verse the word *adulteress* simply means anything that tempts us to sin. Maybe for you, it's sitting in math class and seeing the answer key to the test on the teachers desk and being tempted to look. Or maybe it's hanging out with your friends and being tempted to talk ugly about another person.

This verse says sin is smooth like oil and appealing like honey! But, in the end, sin is as bitter as "gall" and as sharp as a double-edged sword. Say what?

Think about it this way. If you saw a spoonful of cherry cough syrup that smelled oh-so-good, you might think it would taste oh-so-good. Unless you've had cough syrup before and then you know better! It smells appealing, but the taste doesn't match the smell!

Gall is actually a plant from which bitter-tasting juice is made and used in medicine! Sin might seem like it's something good and right and appealing, but in the end, it will actually hurt you!

Proverbs 2

Proverbs 2:1 My child, listen to me and treasure my instructions.

Proverbs 2:2 Tune your ears to wisdom, and concentrate on understanding.

Proverbs 2:3 Cry out for insight and understanding.

Proverbs 2:4 Search for them as you would for lost money or hidden treasure.

Proverbs 2:5 Then you will understand what it means to fear the LORD, and you will gain knowledge of God.

Proverbs 2:6 For the LORD grants wisdom! From his mouth come knowledge and understanding.

Proverbs 2:7 He grants a treasure of good sense to the godly. He is their shield, protecting those who walk with integrity.

Proverbs 2:8 He guards the paths of justice and protects those who are faithful to him.

Proverbs 2:9 Then you will understand what is right, just, and fair, and you will know how to find the right course of action every time.

Have you ever lost something and torn through your house looking for it? Maybe it was a birthday card from your Aunt Susie with money tucked inside. Or a special piece of jewelry you could have sworn you put back in your jewelry box. It's a pretty yucky feeling especially if you don't end up finding what you were looking for. I know that feeling because I lost something about twenty years ago that was worth $6000! And get this: It didn't even belong to me!

I used to sell big, sparkly diamonds—you know, like the kind you see in wedding rings. I was always very careful when I showed my customer a loose diamond. Each one comes wrapped tightly in white tissue paper folded into a small rectangle. I would gently unfold the tissue wrapping and place the diamond in tweezers that would hold it tightly in place. I would then hold it up in front of the light so my customer could see the brilliance of the stone. And that is exactly what I was doing one day when showing a beautiful diamond to a customer when he said, "That's the one. I'll take it!" He paid for the diamond, but I kept it so I could take it to my craftsman. A craftsman sets the diamond on a pretty band, so the ring is ready to go with the wedding proposal. My customer was planning to propose that weekend, so I called my craftsman and told him I would stop by with the diamond later that day.

After my son woke-up from his nap, I loaded him in the car and grabbed the diamond on my way out the door. The diamond was still wrapped in its original white tissue paper and I placed it in a brown lunch sack, folded the lunch sack over and then put it in the baby's diaper bag. Once I arrived, I got out of my car and put the diaper bag in the bottom basket of my baby stroller. I put my son in the stroller and gently lifted the stroller over the curb and onto the sidewalk. I had to weave the stroller in and out of a crowd that was beginning to gather outside a popular restaurant near my craftsman's studio. After making my way down the long, winding sidewalk leading to the back of the complex where the studio was located, I finally arrived. My craftsman was expecting me and after commenting on how big the baby had gotten since I was last by, she said, "OK, let's see what you've got." I reached down to the basket in the stroller and pulled out the diaper bag containing the lunch sack with the diamond, but the sack WAS GONE!

My heart was racing as I dumped all the contents of the diaper bag out onto the floor, praying I would see the brown lunch sack. When I quickly realized the sack simply wasn't there, my craftsman suggested I go back to the car and retrace my exact steps. She said she would watch the baby and off I raced, praying the whole way back to my car that I would locate the sack with the $6000 diamond in it. Finally I arrived at my car and immediately dropped to my knees and looked under the car to see if maybe it fell out of the bag when I removed it from the car. Nothing was there. I looked up and realized that many of the people who were waiting a few yards away in front of the busy restaurant were now staring at me.

I tried not to pay attention to the stares and began retracing my steps from the car to the sidewalk. I followed the exact path the stroller took and then suddenly, out of the corner of my eye, I saw it . . . a brown paper lunch sack sitting right next to the curb just inches away from the crowd of people! I rushed over and picked up the folded sack and prayed it was the lunch sack with the diamond in it. When I tore into the sack, my hands were shaking with hopeful anticipation. *"Please Lord, let the diamond be in here,"* I mumbled under my breath. And then I saw it: The rectangular shape of the neatly folded white tissue paper with the diamond tucked safely inside! It must have fallen out of the diaper bag when I popped the stroller up over the curb onto the sidewalk. I let out a huge sigh of relief and raced back to the studio with the sack containing the diamond in hand.

On the way home I thought about how close I came to losing a valuable treasure. Proverbs 2:2–4 says, *"Tune your ears to wisdom, and concentrate on understanding. Cry out for insight and understanding. Search for them as you would for lost money or hidden treasure."* As valuable as that diamond was, it doesn't begin to compare to the priceless treasure of wisdom. God tells us to search for it as we would lost money or treasure. Which by the way, is exactly what you are doing when you're reading this book. You are taking a journey into a book in the Bible that is full of the treasure of God's wisdom. Who needs diamonds when you can have that kind of treasure?!

As valuable as that diamond was, it doesn't begin to compare to the priceless treasure of wisdom.

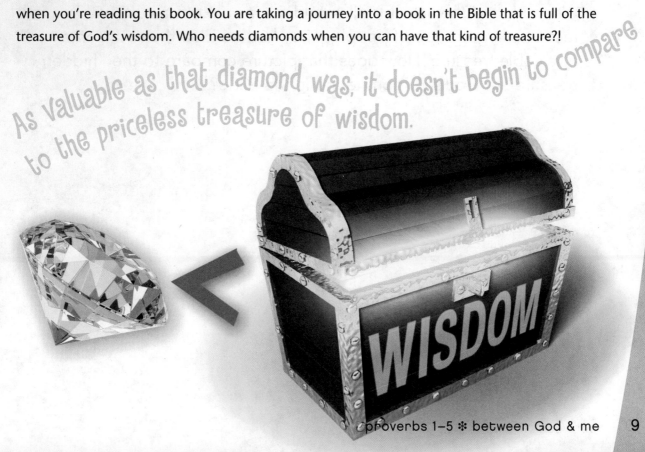

JUST BETWEEN US

1. Count the number of times you see the word "treasure" in the Proverbs 2 verses.

2. Can you think of a time when you lost something valuable? What was it and why was it valuable? Did you ever find it?

3. Why do you think most people don't bother to search for the hidden treasure of God's wisdom?

4. Write down Proverbs 2:9. What does the Lord say will help you find the "right course of action every time" (see Proverbs 2:6–7)?

5. When I found the valuable diamond, it was next to a curb within a few feet of a large group of people. They had no idea the sack contained a valuable treasure. How does that picture compare to the "hidden treasure" of God's wisdom found in the Bible?

PSSST, GOD!

Take a minute to talk to God and ask Him to give you wisdom and understanding when you read His Word. Thank Him for offering such a valuable and priceless treasure.

Do you like taking tests? For me, it depends. If it's an essay test, or any kind of test where I can explain my answer, I do like taking tests. But, when it comes to True/False or multiple-choice tests, I never do very well. If I look at the answers long enough, I can almost convince myself the wrong answer might be the right answer . . . especially when your teacher gives you trick questions to try to confuse you!

Sometimes the Bible can be confusing, but God is clear in His Word about who He is and how He expects us to live in this great big world. **LIES to Wise** will test your knowledge of what Scripture says in Proverbs. This is the kind of test where all the "answers" are false (lies) and you have to make them true. Look up the verse to find the real answers and rewrite the **LIES** below and make them **Wise**.

LIE: *Don't listen to your parents because they don't really know what they're talking about. (Proverbs 1:8)*

to Wise: _____

LIE: *I should trust God with part of my heart and trust my best friend with the other part. (Proverbs 3:5)*

to Wise: _____

LIE: *The Lord disciplines us because He doesn't like us. (Proverbs 3:12)*

to Wise: _____

LIE: *If I leave God's path, He won't know about it. (Proverbs 5:21)*

to Wise: _____

LIE: *Wisdom is something you learn in school or in a textbook. (Proverbs 2:6)*

to Wise: _____

LIE: *If my friends try to entice (tempt) me, I should go along with it. (Proverbs 1:10)*

to Wise: _____

LIE: *If I follow God, He will make my paths look like a zig-zaggy maze. (Proverbs 3:6)*

to Wise: _____

LIE: *The way of the wicked is bright and hopeful. (Proverbs 4:19)*

to Wise: _____

Proverbs 3

Proverbs 3:1 My child, never forget the things I have taught you. Store my commands in your heart,

Proverbs 3:2 for they will give you a long and satisfying life.

Proverbs 3:3 Never let loyalty and kindness get away from you! Wear them like a necklace; write them deep within your heart.

Proverbs 3:4 Then you will find favor with both God and people, and you will gain a good reputation.

When I was in grade school, my best friend gave me the coolest gift for my birthday. It was one of those necklaces that had half of a heart hanging on a chain. At first I was kind of confused over why it wasn't a whole heart, but then she pulled out another necklace with the other half of the heart on it! When you put the two heart pieces together, they formed a whole heart that had "Best Friends" engraved on it. She would wear one and I would wear the other!

Best Friends Forever?

Proverbs 3:3

never let loyalty and kindness get away from you!

Wear them like a necklace;

write them deep within your heart.

I can't remember who lost their necklace first, but it didn't really matter. The following year we ended up in two different homeroom classes and with a new homeroom came a new best friend. The necklace couldn't solve the problem of not seeing each other every day in class, the lunchroom, and P.E. We still hung out from time to time, but since we didn't see each other during school hours, our "best friend" status fizzled to just "friend" status.

While having a best friend seems to be a concern to many girls, the bigger concern should be what kind of friend we are to others. Proverbs 3:3 reminds us to wear loyalty and kindness like a necklace and write them deep within our hearts. Unfortunately you're going to meet girls who aren't wearing that necklace. You are bound to cross paths with girls who love to gossip, bully, cause drama, and sometimes, just be mean for no reason at all.

I often hear from girls your age who are in friendships with girls who cause them pain. Many of them say they put up with drama, meanness, and gossip because they don't have any other friends. If you are in a friendship that causes you more tears than joy, get out! Pray and ask God to bring a new friend your way who practices loyalty and kindness. You deserve someone who appreciates the wonderful person God created you to be. You might even have to tell your mother you need a new friend or two and ask her to help you think of new girls you can invite over who will treat you better.

Oh, and one last thing. Make sure you are wearing loyalty and kindness like a necklace. Proverbs 3:4 reminds us that you will find favor with both God and people and gain a good reputation. *Reputation* is a word that basically means the opinion others have of you. Would others describe you as "loyal" or "kind"? A true friendship is one where both girls are wearing the necklace of "loyalty and kindness." And trust me, that's by far, more valuable than the "best friends" heart necklace my friend gave me. If you write "loyalty" and "kindness" deep within your heart, you won't have to worry about losing it.

JUST BETWEEN US

1. Do you have a friend who wears the necklace of "loyalty and kindness" and acts like a true friend?

2. If you answered no to the above question, can you think of someone you may know who is loyal and kind? Is it possible to invite them over?

3. Would others describe your reputation as loyal and/or kind? If not, what can you do to become a better friend?

4. Using the idea of the necklace my friend gave me with the matching half heart, draw a picture of what the necklace of loyalty and kindness might look like if it were a real piece of jewelry.

PSSST, GOD!

Take a minute to talk to God and ask Him to help you be a good friend who practices loyalty and kindness. Also ask Him to help you find other girls who are practicing loyalty and kindness.

IN THIS CORNER
HIGH WAY vs MY WAY

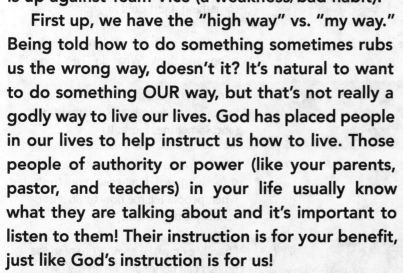

Have you ever seen a boxing match? OK, well maybe not a WHOLE match, but you've probably at least caught a glimpse of the boxing ring with two boxers, one in each corner, right? "In this corner" was created to pick out some things we have learned in Proverbs and point out the opposite truth. Just like the two boxers in the ring are on different teams, these ideas or behaviors are opposites (i.e., wisdom vs. folly). Proverbs teaches us about wise behaviors, so use "In this corner" to help discover some areas where you aren't on the right team! Team Virtue (a good quality) is up against Team Vice (a weakness/bad habit).

First up, we have the "high way" vs. "my way." Being told how to do something sometimes rubs us the wrong way, doesn't it? It's natural to want to do something OUR way, but that's not really a godly way to live our lives. God has placed people in our lives to help instruct us how to live. Those people of authority or power (like your parents, pastor, and teachers) in your life usually know what they are talking about and it's important to listen to them! Their instruction is for your benefit, just like God's instruction is for us!

Let's see what team you're on! On the next page, rate yourself by selecting a number that best describes how you typically behave. The closer you circle a number to the left (or 1) means you are most like the sentence on the left. The same is true of the right hand side. A score of 5 or 6 would mean that you fall somewhere in the middle.

TEAM VIRTUE vs TEAM VICE

STAR PLAYER: HIGH WAY

STAR PLAYER: MY WAY

Team Virtue		Team Vice
I always read the directions on tests or homework assignments.	1 2 3 4 5 6 7 8 9 10	I usually get things wrong on tests and homework because I didn't read the instructions.
When Mom offers help while I'm deciding what to order at a restaurant, I listen.	1 2 3 4 5 6 7 8 9 10	When Mom tells me I won't like something at a restaurant, I pick it anyway.
When given a warning about not doing something, I listen.	1 2 3 4 5 6 7 8 9 10	When someone tells me not to do something, I just do it anyway.
I pay attention to teachers when they tell me things I need to work on.	1 2 3 4 5 6 7 8 9 10	I ignore teachers who tell me to work on things and think "What do THEY know?"
If my parents tell me to put on a jacket because it's cold, I listen.	1 2 3 4 5 6 7 8 9 10	If my parents tell me to put on a jacket, I usually decide to brave it without one (and sometimes regret it).
When I'm frustrated because I can't do something well, I find somebody to walk me through it and follow their steps.	1 2 3 4 5 6 7 8 9 10	When I'm frustrated because I can't do something well, I get even more frustrated when people tell me how to do it and I usually ignore them.
I make an effort to learn the Bible, God's ultimate instruction manual.	1 2 3 4 5 6 7 8 9 10	I hardly ever make an effort to read the Bible. I can figure out life on my own.
If Mom tells me it's not smart to purchase something, I listen.	1 2 3 4 5 6 7 8 9 10	If Mom says not to buy something, I usually buy it anyway.
While playing sports, if my coach gives me pointers, I listen and change how I'm playing.	1 2 3 4 5 6 7 8 9 10	When playing sports, I ignore my coach's pointers and usually keep doing it my way.
In church, I pay attention to lessons and try to learn about how to live a godly life.	1 2 3 4 5 6 7 8 9 10	In church, I usually wiggle and squirm, counting the minutes until it's over.

Now add up all your circled numbers and see how you scored . . .

If you scored between 10 and 39, you're a star student! When it comes to listening to advice of those in authority, you make an A++. You understand the wisdom of listening to those who have been there, done that. Instead of letting your own plans and desires win out, you make wise choices and usually benefit from them!

If you scored between 40 and 70, you're headed to the back of the class! If you're not careful, you'll constantly find yourself in frustrating situations that could easily have been avoided. Even though you sometimes take the good advice of others, you still have a stubborn streak that causes you to choose your own way. Next time someone in authority (like a parent or teacher) gives you instruction, try listening to their advice and giving it a try. Even though someone's advice may not always work out, we should be open to it!

DOWN FOR THE COUNT!

If you scored between 71 and 100, then girl, you are detention bound! When you hear advice, you tend to quickly do the opposite. Instead of caring about what might be wise, you prefer to blaze your own trail, which often leads to heartache. God has placed authority figures in your life for a reason, so start opening those ears and your heart!

Proverbs 4

Proverbs 4:23 Above all else, guard your heart, for it affects everything you do.

Proverbs 4:24 Avoid all perverse talk; stay far from corrupt speech.

Proverbs 4:25 Look straight ahead, and fix your eyes on what lies before you.

Proverbs 4:26 Mark out a straight path for your feet; then stick to the path and stay safe.

Proverbs 4:27 Don't get sidetracked; keep your feet from following evil.

Did you know?

- Your heart was the first organ to begin functioning when you were in your mother's womb.
- Your heart is the hardest working muscle in your body.
- Your heart is approximately the same size as your fist.
- Your heart beats: 100,000 times a day, 35 million times a year, and 2.5 billion times a lifetime (on average).
- In an average lifetime, the heart pumps 1 million barrels of blood.
- Enough power is generated in the heart in one day to drive a car 20 miles.
- The human heart can create enough pressure that it could squirt blood at a distance of thirty feet.

OK, so I know that last fact was a bit gross, but c'mon, you have to admit— that's pretty cool! Obviously it's important to take care of your heart so you can live a long and healthy life. If someone doesn't take good care of their heart, they can get heart disease. Heart disease can lead to a heart attack and a heart attack can lead to death. But the good news is that heart disease can be prevented. Doctors recommend two things: diet and exercise.

So, why am I telling you this? You're young and it's not like you're at risk of heart disease, but believe it or not, you are at risk of another kind of heart attack—a spiritual heart attack. The Bible says to "guard your heart for it affects everything you do." But what exactly does that mean to guard our heart? Basically it means to protect your heart from things that could cause damage and affect your relationship with God— the One who knit your heart together. And amazingly, the same two things that doctors recommend to help prevent a real-live heart attack, are the same two things Christians can do to prevent a spiritual heart attack: diet and exercise.

Diet Garbage in, Garbage out!

Have you ever heard that saying, "Garbage in, garbage out"? It basically means whatever you put into your heart will affect your actions. For example, if you only eat junk food and never eat healthy foods, your body will not be as healthy as it should be. And just like food can affect the physical condition of your heart, TV shows, music, movies, friends, and other influences can affect the spiritual condition of your heart.

I often tell teenage girls who really want a boyfriend that if they're not careful, it can cause damage to their hearts, spiritually. If they get too focused on their boyfriend and he's all they think about, then they won't be as close in their relationship with God, right?

Exercise

Just like it's important to exercise regularly to have a healthy heart, it's also important to exercise spiritually to have a healthy heart. Spiritual exercise includes prayer (talking to God just like you would a close friend) and reading your Bible. Sometimes it's hard for girls to read their Bibles regularly because they don't always understand what they are reading. That's why I'm covering the whole book of Proverbs in this issue of *Between*. You are actually learning to study your Bible by reading this book. Better yet, you are exercising your heart!

So, what do you say? Is your heart in good shape? If not, it's not too late to change your diet (be careful what you watch, listen to, and who you hang out with) and start exercising (praying and reading your Bible)! And if you ask me, that's way better for you than doing a thousand-kadrillion jumping jacks in gym class. Just don't tell your P.E. teacher I said that!

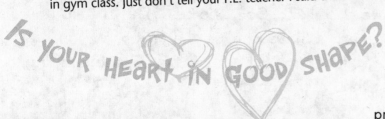

IS YOUR HEART IN GOOD SHAPE?

JUST BETWEEN US

1. Just for fun, draw a picture of a "guarded heart."
(Hint: Think of maybe a fence that guards a garden or back yard)

2. Can you think of a TV show, movie, or song that you saw or heard where you were left feeling uncomfortable and like it wasn't good for your heart?

3. How might you change your daily diet to have a healthier heart (spiritually)?

4. What are some ways you are exercising your heart (spiritually)?
(Ex: Read Bible, pray, go to church)

5. How might you need to improve your daily "work-out" plan to keep your heart in good shape?

PSSST, GOD!

Take a minute to talk to God and ask Him to help you guard your heart. What's cool is that even as you are praying and asking Him to help you, you are exercising your heart at that very moment!

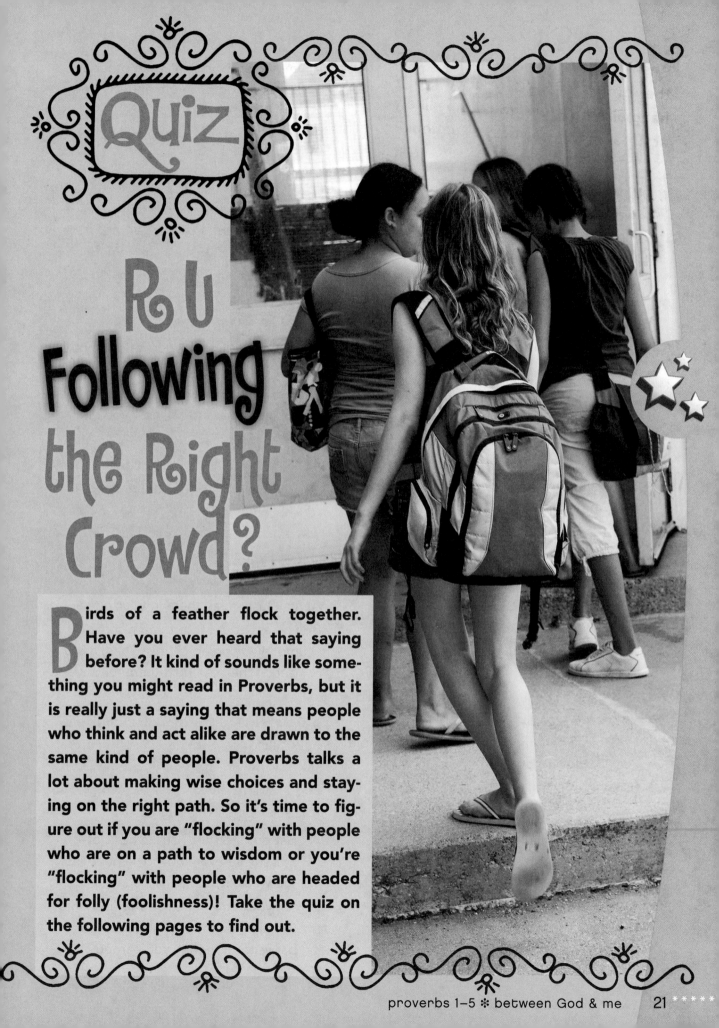

Quiz

R U Following the Right Crowd?

Birds of a feather flock together. Have you ever heard that saying before? It kind of sounds like something you might read in Proverbs, but it is really just a saying that means people who think and act alike are drawn to the same kind of people. Proverbs talks a lot about making wise choices and staying on the right path. So it's time to figure out if you are "flocking" with people who are on a path to wisdom or you're "flocking" with people who are headed for folly (foolishness)! Take the quiz on the following pages to find out.

Answer these questions based on the group of girls you currently hang around. How would they likely act/react in these sticky situations?

1. After a long week at school, your mom drops you off at a movie to meet some of your friends. You had mom's approval to see the newest PG tween movie that isn't supposed to have any bad parts. Also, your best friend's big sister who's in college is going to sit with your group. When you greet your friends at the ticket counter they . . .

A) buy tickets for a completely different movie with a PG-13 rating you know your mom would not approve of.

B) follow through with the original plan and buy tickets for the PG movie your mom approved.

2. It's time for gym class and your teacher makes you a team captain for kickball. As you take turns picking members, your first pick is a girl who usually doesn't get picked until last. Your friends . . .

A) stare at you like "why on EARTH did you pick HER and not ME?"

B) smile and nod at your sweet example of loving others.

3. You are at Olivia's house for her birthday sleepover. She has invited one of her cousins, who no one really knows. Her cousin is a little odd and sometimes says some strange things. When she leaves the room the first time your friends . . .

A) immediately look at each other and start to giggle, laugh, and say how weird she is.

B) act as if nothing was different.

4. It's 4th period English class and you totally forgot to study for the quiz. Your friends are sitting near you in class and see the panic on your face when you realize it's Quiz Day. In the middle of the quiz, the teacher leaves the room. Your friends . . .

A) immediately look your way to mouth you the answers.

B) keep to themselves and catch up with you after class to ask how you did.

5. While browsing your favorite store at the local mall with one of your friends while your mom shops nearby, you see some really cool, hair clips that are too expensive for you. Your friend suggests . . .

A) you just sneak them in your purse.

B) you ask your Mom to earn some money by doing chores. Then, ask the clerk if they can hold them for a week.

6. Your older sister bought the coolest new shirt last weekend. You borrow it for the end of the year school party, and accidentally spill red punch all over it. Your friends tell you to . . .

A) just put the shirt back in her closet and she'll never know. The next time she wears it, she'll think she stained it.

B) tell your sister you're sorry and offer to help clean it or replace it with babysitting money you earned.

7. You and your friends are invited to Laura's sleepover party on Friday. She's a sweet girl and you all accepted her invitation. Then, the next day Natalie invites you and your best friend to her sleepover on Friday. Natalie is the coolest girl in the grade ABOVE yours. Your best friend suggests you go . . .

A) to Natalie's house and tell Laura something came up. Surely she'll understand.

B) to Laura's since you had already committed to her and thank Natalie for inviting you.

8. Your group is given an opportunity to take part in a service project on a Saturday helping less fortunate people. Your group of friends . . .

A) go, but gripe about having to be there and look for ways to kill time by taking looooong bathroom breaks.

B) go and enjoy the experience serving together.

How did U score?

Caution: Danger Ahead! (5 or more A's)

Stop. Do not pass go, do not collect $200. You are not following the right crowd! You choose friends who lead you down the wrong path. Remove yourself from groups of friends who pressure you to compromise your values or base their opinion of you on whether you will follow them on the path to foolishness. True friendships will encourage you to seek God and make right choices. Proverbs 17:17 says *"A friend loves at all times"* (NIV). Keep this in mind when you find yourself with the wrong crowd and their actions don't look very loving!

Stuck at the fork in the road (Equal number of A's and B's)

You seem to hang with friends on both paths. It might be time to take a closer look at the group that encourages you to make bad choices. Is it really worth it? While it's always good to be a light to those girls, make sure your closest friends are on the right path.

On the straight and narrow (5 or more B's)

You are on the right path! You see the value of choosing friends who are like-minded and do not compromise your values. These friends will encourage you to do what is right and help you stay on the right path.

Proverbs 5

HEY, LOOK EVERYBODY! She's telling a lie about her teacher!

Proverbs 5:21 For the LORD sees clearly what a man does, examining every path he takes.

She's copying the answers onto her homework.

Imagine if one day at school the principal announced on the loud speaker that there were hidden cameras all around the school. Now imagine that the principal said someone would be watching TV monitors in a control room throughout the day and writing down students' names when they misbehaved. Then, at the end of the day, the control room operators would turn the list of names into the principal and each name would be announced over the loud speaker, noting the offenses committed. That would be crazy, right?

Well, believe it or not, the police department in one wacky British town did something similar in an effort to cut back on crime. They set up 158 cameras around the city and fitted seven of them with loud speakers. Control room operators would watch their assigned area and step in if there was any trouble. One young man who lived in the town was riding his bike and he pedaled into an area of a park where bikes were not allowed.

All of a sudden a loud voice came from one of the speakers overhead and said, "Would the young man on the bike please get off and walk as he is riding in a pedestrian area?" The surprised boy stopped and looked around, confused, and unsure where the voice came from.

She's on a chat site instead of doing her work!

She's texting on her cell phone in class!

When he realized the mystery voice was referring to him, he immediately got off his bike and walked it away from the park area, his face bright red with embarrassment as surprised onlookers watched him.

Proverbs 5:21 tells us God has the ability to see everything we do. Nothing is hidden from His sight. Fortunately He doesn't sit in a control room all day and scream at us over a loud speaker when we misbehave. Or take our names down and turn it into our parents! He gives us the freedom to choose our paths—even when we decide to go off course. He is patient and loving, nudging us to get back on track when we stray. I don't know about you, but knowing God loves me that way makes me want to obey Him. It would be hard to love a God who yelled at me every time I messed up.

It kind of reminds me of my 6th grade math teacher, Mrs. Cooper, who caught me passing a note to one of my friends one day in class. She intercepted the note and proceeded to read it out loud to the class. It was embarrassing enough since I told my friend I thought Steve Miller was super-cute and he was sitting right there on the front row. But here's the worst part: I also said something about Mrs. Cooper being the meanest teacher in the entire universe. After she read my to the class, she folded it back up, handed it to me, and sent me to the office to read the note to the principal. Joy.

God has the ability to see everything we do

My punishment, you may wonder? The principal made me write "I will not pass notes in class. I will show respect to my teacher." one hundred times. Ouch. I mean, oh sure, I probably deserved to get in trouble, but did Mrs. Cooper have to embarrass me in front of the entire class? And in front of Steve Miller?! So yeah, I still think she is the meanest teacher in the entire universe, but you can bet I wasn't going to write it in a note after that! In fact, let's hope she doesn't read it in this book—I'm still afraid she might hunt me down and try to send me to the office!

I will not pass notes in class. I will show respect to my teacher.
I will not pass notes in class. I will show respect to my teacher.
I will not pass notes in class. I will show respect to my teacher.
I will not pass notes in class. I will show respect to my teacher.
I will not pass notes in class. I will show respect to my teacher.
I will not pass notes in class. I will show respect to my teacher.

LOOK!! She's cheating on her exam!

1. Stop for a minute and think about this past week. Can you think of something you did wrong? Maybe you talked back to your mother, gossiped about a friend, or told a lie to your brother. What was it?

2. Do you think God knew it when you sinned at the time?

3. How would you feel if God shouted at you from the heavens and pointed out what you did in front of your family and friends?

4. Would it make you want to be closer to God? Yes or No

5. Can you think of a time when someone (parent, teacher, etc.) was patient with you when you made a mistake and corrected you in a loving manner? If so, who was it and what happened?

Take a minute to talk to God. Thank Him for being patient and loving even when you stray from His path. Ask Him to send loving reminders when you stray to nudge you back on the right path.

Proverbial Dictionary/Concordance

You may come across some words in the book of Proverbs that need some explanation. If you have a mom like mine, she'll make you look up the word in the dictionary if you don't know what it means, even if she knows what it means! Ugh!

Hopefully this dictionary will help you understand some of the harder words you come across in Proverbs. If you run across others that aren't on this list, there's space to add them at the bottom of the chart. You can ask your mom, dad, or Sunday school teacher for some help OR you can look them up in a dictionary on your own. Keep in mind that not all Bible translations contain the same exact words in a Bible verse, but most of the words below show up in many of the translations.

Oh, and in case you're wondering . . . if you see a Bible verse address like for example Proverbs 4:5, the first number before the ":" is the chapter, and the number after the ":" is the verse. So, for Proverbs 4:5, it is referring to Proverbs, chapter 4 (big number in your Bible), verse 5 (smaller number in your Bible.)

Word	Definition	Where to find it in Proverbs
Adultery	In Proverbs, this word describes the act of loving something else more than God. Sometimes it is used to describe a person (adulteress) who entices you to sin or lure you away from the things of God. (See article on Proverbs 1 to learn more about staying away from those who entice you to sin.)	3:16–17; Chapter 5; Chapter 6; Chapter 7
Discretion	To use good judgment or make good choices when making decisions from day-to-day.	2:11; 3:21; 10:31; 11:22
Ensnared	To be lured in and trapped. An example sentence might read: The mouse was ensnared by the mousetrap when he smelled the cheese. He didn't have much "discretion" did he?	6:2; 22:25
Fear of the Lord	This does not mean to be afraid of God. It means to have an awe and wonder for how awesome God is!	9:10; 19:23; 31:30
Folly	This is another word for foolishness. It means a lack of good sense or judgment that leads to foolish actions.	Chapter 6; Chapter 9; 15:14
Foolishness/Fool	Showing folly through poor judgment and foolish actions. Not making the right choices.	1:7; 10:18; 12:15; 17:28
Humility	The opposite of being prideful or being a bragger. If you are humble, you understand that you are nothing without Jesus.	11:2; 18:12;, 22:4
Instruction	A set of rules to follow. The Bible is our instruction manual for life.	4:13; 8:33; 16:20; 19:27
Insight	The act of understanding something. Since God inspired the Bible (wrote it through men), we can gain insight from Him.	2:3; 4:5; 21:30
Integrity	Total honesty and sincerity. Acting the same in private when no one is watching as you would in public when you are around other people. Keeping your word to someone no matter what.	10:9; 11:3; 13:6
Knowledge	To have information about something that is gained by learning or experience.	1:7; 2:6; 8:12; 9:10; 10:14; 15:7; 23:12; 24:5
Pride	A feeling of self-importance. Having a higher opinion of oneself than one ought to!	8:13; 13:10; 16:18
Prudence	Using caution and good sense. Getting in the habit of thinking before you speak/act.	8:5; 8:12; 12:23; 15:5
Righteous	That which is right. To Christians, it also refers to the holiness of Jesus, which God exchanged for our sin when Jesus died on the cross. Because of Jesus, we are seen as righteous, or pure, in God's eyes. Pretty amazing, huh?!	Chapter 10; 10:29; 11:19; 12:5; 18:10
Trust	Belief in the character, ability, strength, or truth of someone or something.	3:5–6; 22:19
Understanding	To get the meaning of something. To "get it."	10:23; 11:12
Upright	Living by high moral (godly) standards; making wise choices.	2:21; 14:2
Wise	Describes someone who practices wisdom. (See below)	Throughout entire book of Proverbs!
Wisdom	Using knowledge to make good decisions, and honoring God by using the knowledge we gain from reading His word (the Bible).	Throughout entire book of Proverbs!

Listen to me! For I have excellent things to tell you.

Don't talk too much, for it fosters sin.

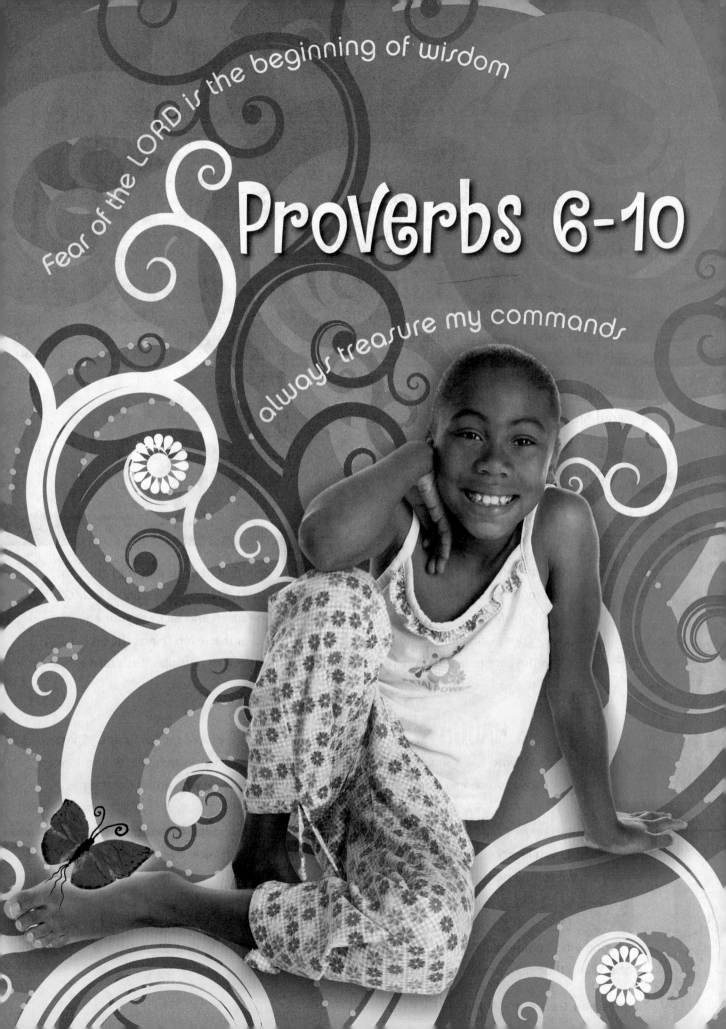

Proverbs 6

Proverbs 6:16 There are six things the LORD hates—no, seven things he detests:

Proverbs 6:17 haughty eyes, a lying tongue, hands that kill the innocent,

Proverbs 6:18 a heart that plots evil, feet that race to do wrong,

Proverbs 6:19 a false witness who pours out lies, a person who sows discord among brothers.

I'm betting that by now you've had at least one RMG encounter. And trust me, you're lucky if you've only had one. What's an RMG you may wonder? RMG = Really Mean Girl. It's a fact of life that girls can be mean and tacky at your age, but how does God feel about mean girls? If you read over the seven things the Bible tells us the Lord hates, most of them describe the games mean girls play. Let's take a look at them:

1. HAUGHTY EYES
Haughty is just a fancy word for "snobbish." Someone who has haughty eyes acts like they are better than everyone else and looks down on people. Sometimes they like to leave out people who aren't like them.

2. A LYING TONGUE
Have you ever known someone who has to be right all the time and they'll even lie about things just to come across as a know-it-all? After awhile, lying becomes such a habit for the person they often start to believe their own lies!

3. HANDS THAT KILL THE INNOCENT
Well, hopefully, you don't know anyone who committed this sin! Even so, a mean girl often enjoys hurting the hearts of others and killing their self-confidence.

4. A HEART THAT PLOTS EVIL

Basically this kind of girl is a troublemaker and is always coming up with a new plan to break the rules.

5. FEET THAT RACE TO DO WRONG

This girl is like the girl above who is looking for trouble except she races out to do it, which makes her more of a follower. In other words, she is happy to go along with other girls who are "plotting evil." Do you know girls like that?

6. A FALSE WITNESS WHO POURS OUT LIES

This person is worse than the person who has a bad habit of telling lies. This person actually makes things up about other people and spreads it around. Do you know someone who loves to gossip about other people?

7. A PERSON WHO SOWS DISCORD AMONG BROTHERS

The word *sows* means to "spread" like you would do when scattering seed in a garden. The word *discord* means "disagreement." If you put both words together, you have a girl who likes to "spread disagreements" around. Do you know someone like this who loves to cause drama?

The truth is, we have all probably committed one or more of the above sins. God forgives us when we sin, but the verses above remind us He takes mean-girl behaviors very seriously. One of the things I hear often that makes my heart hurt for you girls, is that many of the mean girls are in our churches! Christian girls should know better than to commit the sins above and act like it's no big deal.

However, it's important to remember that giving to the church doesn't make you a Christian. If you are around a girl who commits one or more of the above sins on a regular basis, it might be a good idea to find a new friend (or group of friends) until or unless you see an improvement. Pray that God will open her eyes to the fact she is committing one or more of the sins on God's Top Seven Most-Hated Sins list. Oh, and you might not want to point that fact out to her. Maybe just pass her this copy of *Between* when you're done reading it and dog-ear this page!

JUST BETWEEN US

1. Describe a recent mean-girl encounter. Which of the sins above did the mean girl commit? (If you are discussing this in a group, please don't use names!)

2. Which of the sins on page 30 do you struggle with the most? Do you struggle every now and then, or is it more of a habit?

3. If it's more of a habit, do you think you could be behaving like a mean girl?

4. What do you think about the idea of staying away from girls who regularly commit three or more of the sins on the list above? Is there anyone you might need to stay away from? (Again, please don't list any names if you are doing this in a group.)

Pray and ask God to show you if you have been behaving like a mean girl. There might be someone you need to apologize to in an effort to make things right. Now, pray for any girls who come to mind who have been behaving like mean girls. Ask God to change their hearts and help them see how serious He is about sin.

PSSST, GOD!

SAY WHAT?

Go to the ant, you sluggard; consider its ways and be wise! It has no commander, no overseer or ruler, yet it stores its provisions in summer and gathers its food at harvest. (Proverbs 6:6-8 NIV)

Have you ever been called a sluggard? Do you even know what it is? If you look it up in the dictionary, you might find a definition like this: a person who is habitually inactive or lazy. *Habitually* basically means "all the time." So, a sluggard is someone who is in the habit of being lazy all or most of the time. For instance, say you were supposed to set the table for dinner and instead and you chose to watch TV. When your family sits down and discovers they have no silverware, they may call you a sluggard for not doing your job! Even worse, you might get grounded from that TV when Mom or Dad figures out what distracted you from doing your job.

These verses above talk about an insect we can learn from if we are lazy. We should watch how ants operate to learn how to be wise and productive. Ants are really remarkable creatures. Have you ever noticed how teeny they are, and yet, somehow they carry crumbs and other things almost twice their size over rocks, trees, grass, park benches, and more just to get to their home? They are unbelievably hard workers and don't even have to be told to clean their room! Okay, so maybe they don't have rooms, but they do work without being told. Proverbs 6:6–8 says that even without a commander or ruler, ants know it is wise to work during the harvest and save up food while it's there! So, consider the ways of the ant and avoid being labeled a sluggard!

WISDOM is learning acquired over a period of time; ability to see beneath the surface of things; good sense.

PRUDENCE is the ability to think ahead when making choices.

KNOWLEDGE is facts or ideas you learn or get by study, observation, or experience.

DISCRETION is the quality of using sound judgment or making good choices.

I, wisdom, dwell together with prudence; I possess knowledge and discretion.
(Proverbs 8:12 NIV)

Now, obviously words don't have a home, but the idea is they all go together. Just like real brothers and sisters, these words are related to each other, but they actually get along quite nicely! They all have the same parent: God and His divine wisdom. From His wisdom you become wise. You learn over a period of time to use the knowledge you've gained from God to exercise discretion (good judgment) and prudence (thinking ahead) to make wise choices.

As vinegar to the teeth and smoke to the eyes, so is a sluggard to those who send him. (Proverbs 10:26 NIV)

Have you ever been camping? If so, I bet you have gathered around a campfire to roast marshmallows. Maybe at some point or another, the breeze caught the smoke from the campfire and blew it right in your face. I hate that feeling! Instead of enjoying your Smore, you end up rubbing your eyes for the rest of the night . . . or even worse, you burn your marshmallow because the smoke blinded your eyes and you can't see it over the fire anymore!

This verse says, "like vinegar to the teeth and smoke to the eyes," someone who doesn't take care of their responsibilities is irritating and causes grief. Similar to Proverbs 6:6–8, it is assumed the "sluggard" doesn't complete the task, chore, or errand, given to her. And if that wasn't bad enough, we learn that being a sluggard can actually cause hurt to others!

Proverbs 7

Proverbs 7:1 Follow my advice, my son; always treasure my commands.

Proverbs 7:2 Obey them and live! Guard my teachings as your most precious possession.

Proverbs 7:3 Tie them on your fingers as a reminder. Write them deep within your heart.

Have you ever had a hard time remembering something? Maybe your mom or dad told you about the old fashioned custom of tying a string on your finger to help you remember whatever it is you are supposed to remember. Of course, the problem with that is many people forget the very thing you were supposed to remember when they see the string!

God left us the Bible to remind us of who He is and how much He loves us. The Bible is our instruction manual for living, so it's important that we know what it says. If we are to "treasure God's commands" and "write them deep within our hearts," we must have a plan for reading and under- standing God's Word (the Bible). Hey, stop right now and pat yourself on the back because going through the Proverbs in this issue of *Between* is certainly a good start!

Here's something I occasionally do to help me tie God's teachings on my finger as a reminder and write them deep within my heart:

1. When I'm reading my Bible, I have a pen or highlighter inside my Bible. When I come across a verse that jumps off the page and speaks to my heart, I under- line or highlight it.

2. If it's a really impor- tant verse, I sometimes write it down on a 3x5 note card.

5. I practice saying them out loud when I'm not looking at the note card.

4. I try to read them out loud as often as possible to help me remember them better.

3. I put the note cards somewhere where I will see them on a regular basis and be reminded to read over them. Example: On top of your night stand; tucked inside your Bible; by the computer, etc.

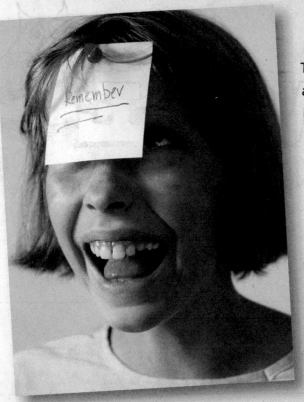

It's kind of like studying for a spelling test. The more you look at the word, write it down, and spell it out loud, the more it begins to sink into your memory. Hopefully, by the time your teacher calls out the words on test day, you will remember how to spell them and make a 100! When we memorize important Bible verses, we tuck them away in our hearts for a day when we may need them. Whether you are scared, nervous, angry, sad, confused, or just flat having a rotten day, God will bring certain Scripture verses to mind to help you. When you store away God's promises in the treasure chest of your mind, you are sure to strike it rich!

JUST BETWEEN US

1. Look back over the Bible verses we have covered in the past seven Proverbs. Is there a verse that really stood out to you? Go ahead and underline it or highlight in this book. (You can also do so in your Bible.)

2. Why did you choose the verse you did?

3. Write it on a note card or a piece of paper and follow my steps above. Try to memorize it over this next week. Say it out loud right now.

PSSST, GOD!

Pray and thank God for His Word. Express to Him how grateful you are to have the Bible to help keep you on His path. Ask Him to show you which verses He wants you to remember when you are reading the Bible.

LIES to WISE

Look up the verses below and rewrite them to change the *LIES* back into **Wise** Bible verses!

LIE: Being diligent is a big waste of time. (Proverbs 10:4)

to Wise: _____

LIE: Those who keep God's ways will be sorry. (Proverbs 8:32)

to Wise: _____

LIE: The fear of the Lord is the beginning of foolishness. (Proverbs 9:10)

to Wise: _____

LIE: Spreading slander (insults) will win you many friends. (Proverbs 10:18)

to Wise: _____

LIE: If you are wise, your wisdom will make a fool of you. (Proverbs 9:12)

to Wise: _____

LIE: The Lord loves a lying tongue (Proverbs 6:17)

to Wise: _____

LIE: Hatred promotes togetherness. (Proverbs 10:12)

to Wise: _____

LIE: To fear the Lord is to love evil. (Proverbs 8:13)

to Wise: _____

Proverbs 8

Proverbs 8:1 Listen as wisdom calls out! Hear as understanding raises her voice!

Proverbs 8:2 She stands on the hilltop and at the crossroads.

Proverbs 8:3 At the entrance to the city, at the city gates, she cries aloud,

Proverbs 8:4 "I call to you, to all of you! I am raising my voice to all people.

Proverbs 8:5 How naive you are! Let me give you common sense. O foolish ones, let me give you understanding

Proverbs 8:6 Listen to me! For I have excellent things to tell you. Everything I say is right,

Proverbs 8:7 for I speak the truth and hate every kind of deception.

Proverbs 8:8 My advice is wholesome and good. There is nothing crooked or twisted in it.

Proverbs 8:9 My words are plain to anyone with understanding, clear to those who want to learn.

Proverbs 8:10 "Choose my instruction rather than silver, and knowledge over pure gold.

Proverbs 8:11 For wisdom is far more valuable than rubies. Nothing you desire can be compared with it.

For I have excellent things to tell you.

Everything I say is right.

My words are plain to anyone with understanding.

STOP

ONE WAY

A few years back I got terribly lost while driving around in a city I wasn't familiar with. I searched and searched for the main road but couldn't find it. The scary thing was, I was on a long stretch of road and there was nowhere to stop and ask for directions along the way. My cell phone was dead and I had no idea what to do. Should I keep on driving in the direction I was headed or should I turn around? I said a prayer and asked God to show me the way home. I was on the verge of tears when suddenly, it hit me: I have a GPS navigational system in my car!

I wasn't in the habit of using it because I'd lived in the same city for more than twenty years, so I always knew where I was going. I pulled over on the side of the road and typed my home address onto the navigation screen. I pressed "start directions" and suddenly a computer voice came on and told me to "turn left and proceed four miles." Step-by-step the voice led me back to the main road, and before long I was on my way home.

The "wisdom" Proverbs 8 talks about is kind of like that navigation system in my car. *"Listen to me! For I have excellent things to tell you. Everything I say is right. . . . My words are plain to anyone with understanding, clear to those who want to learn."* Wisdom comes from God and God makes it available to each and every person. But just like that navigation system, it won't do us any good unless we take advantage of this wonderful gift.

Only when we learn to tune in and listen to the still, quiet voice of God, will we have clear direction in life. God speaks to us through prayer, His Word (the Bible), and sometimes other people who are tuned into His voice. How sad so many people wander through their lives lost and confused, and the whole time God is right there waiting to give them wisdom and understanding. What about you? Are you using God's navigation system? He is ready to give you wisdom and direction, but you have to ask for it!

clear to those who want to learn.

1. Who is the author of wisdom? (Circle one)

The President of the United States

Oprah

God

2. Can you think of a time when you have prayed and asked God to give you direction about something? If so, what was it and how did He answer?

3. In verse 5, what two things can one gain from wisdom?

4. As we seek to know God's heart and read His Word, what does Proverbs 8:9 tell us?

YIELD

PSSST, GOD!

Write a short note below to God and thank Him for some of the benefits of wisdom listed on page 37.

_____

_____

_____

_____

_____

_____

IN THIS CORNER
WISDOM vs FOLLY

You've probably noticed by now that Proverbs is filled with verses about wisdom and folly! Now, let's see which team roster has your name on it! Remember, nobody's perfect, so don't be embarrassed to find you have room to improve in some areas! We all do, even your parents, teachers, and pastors!

Rate yourself by selecting a number that best describes how you typically behave. The closer you circle a number to the left (1–5), the more you behave like the sentence on the left. The closer you circle a number on the right (6–10), the more you behave like the sentence on the right. A score of 5 or 6 would mean that you're somewhere in the middle.

TEAM VIRTUE

VS

TEAM VICE

STAR PLAYER: WISDOM

STAR PLAYER: FOLLY

Wants to do the right thing	1 2 3 4 5 6 7 8 9 10	Usually likes to push the limits
Stays far away from people who do wrong	1 2 3 4 5 6 7 8 9 10	Hangs out with the wrong crowd
Learns God's Word because it is important	1 2 3 4 5 6 7 8 9 10	Doesn't really care about studying the Bible
Listens to advice from wise people like parents or Sunday school teachers	1 2 3 4 5 6 7 8 9 10	Doesn't like to be told how to do things
Trusts that God's way is best	1 2 3 4 5 6 7 8 9 10	Thinks your way is always the best way

Takes responsibility	1 2 3 4 5 6 7 8 9 10	Blames other people
Is a hard worker	1 2 3 4 5 6 7 8 9 10	Is lazy
Holds her tongue	1 2 3 4 5 6 7 8 9 10	Doesn't control her tongue . . . lets anything fly out!
Learns from mistakes and discipline that follows	1 2 3 4 5 6 7 8 9 10	Repeats the same old mistakes
Thinks before acting	1 2 3 4 5 6 7 8 9 10	Acts quickly without thinking.

Now, total up the numbers you circled to see what corner you're in! How did you do?

If you scored between 10 and 39, you tend to lean toward wisdom! Good job. You see the value of making wise choices and understand that it affects every area of your life. You're the winner in this match! Keep up your training!

If you scored between 40 and 70, you are dancing around between wisdom and folly. Depending on the situation, you sometimes choose wisely and other times, choose foolishly. Practice making wise choices this week. Remember: part of being wise is being open to the advice of others!

If you scored between 71 and 100, you lean toward folly (or foolish) decisions! Watch out! The Bible warns that the foolish path does not end in joy or fulfillment. Memorize Proverbs 2:6, *"For the LORD gives wisdom, and from his mouth come knowledge and understanding"* (NIV) and pray for God to reveal His wisdom to you. Then, take two of the statements where you scored an "8 or higher" and write the statement on the "wisdom side" on a note card (the goal you're aiming for) and paste it to your mirror. That way, you'll remember the areas you need to improve. Ask yourself at the end of each week how you are doing. Then switch out the note cards with new ones if there are other areas you need to improve. If you have a teachable heart and you truly desire to improve, you'll get there!

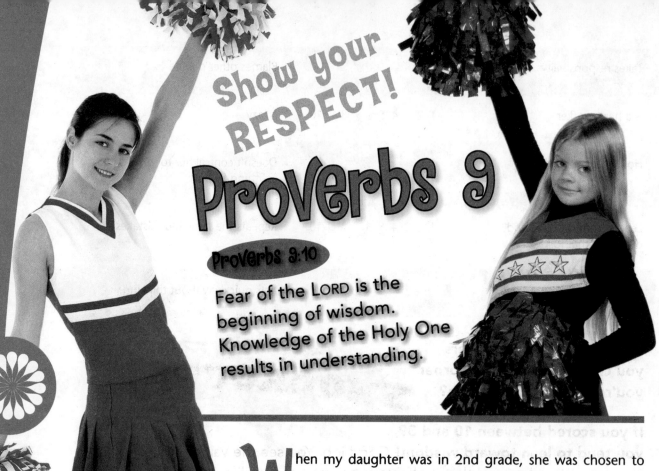

Show your RESPECT!

Proverbs 9

Proverbs 9:10

Fear of the LORD is the beginning of wisdom. Knowledge of the Holy One results in understanding.

When my daughter was in 2nd grade, she was chosen to perform on an award-winning competitive cheer squad for a spring show at a local high school. She was the youngest member of the group and the rest of the girls ranged in age from late elementary through high school. One afternoon when I picked her up from practice, she was especially quiet on the way home. Sensing something was not quite right, I asked her if anything happened during practice that upset her. In response, she burst into tears and said the song they were using in the performance said "something very, very bad," and she was afraid if she told me, I would not allow her to be in the performance.

We were just days shy of the team performing and since my daughter was a flier, I couldn't really take her off the team, so I assured her she could still perform. She went on to tell me some of the words in the song were "sooooooo bad" and she didn't want to say it out loud. Finally I convinced her it was OK in this situation to whisper the words to me. Hesitantly, she leaned over and very quietly whispered the bad words she had heard in the song: "Oh my God." Apparently the song had a part where the phrase was used in a sarcastic tone, and my daughter knew it was wrong to speak God's name in that manner.

I was very proud of my daughter and commended her for responding to the lyrics with a tender "fear of the Lord" at the young age of seven. The "fear of the Lord" Proverbs 9:10 talks about is a reverence and respect for God. If you look up *reverence* in the dictionary, you would find: "A feeling of profound awe and respect and often love; an act showing respect, especially a bow or curtsy." I love that last definition: "a bow or curtsy."

It reminds me of seeing common people bow or curtsy when in the presence of nobility (a king or queen) to show their respect. Yet, how much more does the God of the universe deserve our respect?! While we aren't required to physically bow or curtsy in the Lord's presence, we can at the very least, learn to bow our hearts in honor of our Creator.

Consider the following ways we can bow our hearts and show a proper "fear of the Lord":

Never use the Lord's name in vain. This includes phrases like: "Oh my God!" and "Jesus Christ!" that are often spoken in a disrespectful manner.

Never cut up during prayer time. Focus your attention on the words being spoken.

Participate in singing when worshipping in church rather than merely moving your lips.

Don't talk or fidget during the church service. This also includes writing notes back and forth, checking your cell phone for messages, texting, and other distractions.

How are you doing when it comes to showing "fear of the Lord"? We are all a work in progress, and, fortunately, God is a patient God. Chances are we all have room for improvement when it comes to showing a proper fear of the Lord.

JUST BETWEEN US

Love GOD

1. One of the definitions of *reverence* is "a feeling of profound awe." What is a word girls often use when they like something that contains the word "awe" in it?

2. List three things about God that make you want to say, "Awesome!"

3. In the list of ways we can "bow our hearts" in the red boxes on page 43, what is the area you most struggle with?

4. What are some things you can do to improve in the area you listed in question #3?

PSSST, GOD!

Look over the areas you listed above that need improvement when it comes to showing fear of the Lord. Ask God to send you a gentle reminder when you are getting off track, so you can catch yourself.

R U a liar, liar?

Liar, liar _____ __ ____.

I bet you could finish that sentence! We've all been guilty of lying before and to say we haven't would be . . . well, a lie! Take this quiz and choose the answer that best describes how you might act in the situation.

1. You and your little brother, Davis, sometimes bicker. In the middle of a shoving war, a lamp gets knocked over and breaks. Mom takes you off to the side to find out what happened. You say . . . .

A) "Sorry Mom, Davis and I were fighting and we knocked over a lamp and it broke. It is both our faults."

B) "Mooooom, Davis pushed me into the lamp and it broke!"

C) "Davis broke the lamp, Mom! It was all his fault!"

2. You're walking to the lunchroom when your BFF starts talking about the most amazing pair of really expensive name brand jeans she just bought. As she models them, she says she likes your jeans too and asks where you bought them.

You bought them at Walmart last week, and are slightly embarrassed to tell her. You . . .

A) Smile and say, "Actually, Walmart! Aren't they cute?"

B) Shrug and comment, "I don't really remember."

C) Look straight ahead and quickly say, "Oh, some store in the mall."

3. It's Friday night and your friend Ally has asked you to spend the night. You know Ally has also invited some older girls from her neighborhood to come over who sometimes get into trouble. You know your mom wouldn't be crazy about it if she knew. You . . .

A) Tell your mom anyway and hope she still lets you go.

B) Tell your mom Ally has invited some other friends to come over, but you don't tell her who.

C) Tell your mom Ally has only invited you to spend the night and nothing else.

4. A group of totally cool girls you really want to be friends with are talking about a movie that recently came out they saw over the weekend. Noticing you are semi-listening; they turn to you and ask if you liked the new movie. You haven't seen it because your mom said it was a little too mature and won't allow it. You don't want to get teased about it so you say, . . .

A) "I actually haven't seen it. Did you guys like it?"

B) "I haven't seen it, but I'm planning to see it soon. Tell me all about it!"

C) "Yeah, it was awesome!"

5. Your mom drops you off for school in plenty of time to make it to first period before the bell. On your way to class, you decide to stop in the bathroom with one of your friends and you get to talking and lose track of time. While in there, the late bell rings. You rush to class and tell the teacher . . .

A) "Sorry I'm late. I don't have a good excuse."

B) "I was using the bathroom and couldn't help it."

C) "My mom was a little late dropping me off today."

6. In history class your teacher told you to specifically study the chapter 3 summary to prepare for the test. You forgot and ended up with a D. School policy states that any grade below a C requires a parent's signature. You . . .

A) Ask your mom or dad to sign the test and explain you forgot to study and tell them you're sorry and will do better the next time.

B) Ask your mom or dad to sign the test and tell them almost everyone in class failed, which isn't exactly true.

C) Sign the test yourself. Your parents just won't understand and besides, you would be grounded for life if they knew you failed.

7. Over the summer vacation, you went to camp for a week. The first few nights you were there, your counselor asked all sorts of group questions for everyone to answer. The second night, she asked, "Have you ever met any celebrities?" You technically haven't,

but you know someone who once saw Miley Cyrus from a distance in a grocery store. Almost everyone who answered before you said they have met a celebrity. You say . . .

A) "No! But I have a friend who saw Miley Cyrus at the grocery store!"

B) "Yeah, I sorta met Miley Cyrus through a friend."

C) "Yeah. I've met Miley Cyrus. She shops at my grocery store. I see her all the time. She's so cool."

8. On her way out the door for a meeting, your mom asks you to clean your room because company is coming over for dinner. The minute she leaves, you grab a snack, turn on Wii Sports and play for an hour straight. When Mom gets back, you quickly shut off the Wii before she sees you. When she asks why you haven't cleaned your room you say . . .

A) "Sorry, Mom. I got caught up playing Wii. I'll go do it right now."

B) "I was working out! I was going to do it next, I promise!"

C) "I couldn't find any of the cleaning supplies."

How did U score?

Fireproof!

If you answered mostly A's, your pants are FAR from being on fire! You are an honest Abe (or Abby). You know how to handle situations with grace and honesty. Instead of caring about what others think, you are more concerned about being truthful. Even though honesty is hard to practice, keep it up! Proverbs 24:26 says, "He who gives an honest answer gives a kiss on the lips" (HCSB). So, muah girl, you did good!

Hot and Cold

If you answered mostly B's, that makes you hot and cold. You better watch out, that fire alarm is about to go off. You have a hard time telling the whole truth. Sometimes being honest comes easily, but other times you slip up and lie. Watch out for situations where you know you are tempted to lie (exaggerating in a story, leaving out information you know you shouldn't, bending the truth to sound better, etc.). Even telling half-truths, or not the whole truth, is a lie!

Stop, Drop, and Roll!

If you answered mostly C's, your pants are totally on fire! Stop, drop, and roll! You have some work to do (after you put the fire in your pants out!). You tend to take the easy way out of hard or tempting situations by lying. Take some time and confess this before God. Then, ask a friend or maybe your mom to help you improve by asking you daily or weekly if you have lied about anything. Honesty is always the best policy.

Proverbs 10

Proverbs 10:8 The wise are glad to be instructed, but babbling fools fall flat on their faces.

Proverbs 10:13 Wise words come from the lips of people with understanding, but fools will be punished with a rod.

Proverbs 10:14 Wise people treasure knowledge, but the babbling of a fool invites trouble.

Proverbs 10:19 Don't talk too much, for it fosters sin. Be sensible and turn off the flow!

Proverbs 10:20 The words of the godly are like sterling silver; the heart of a fool is worthless.

Wise girls speak wise words.

They carefully weigh their words before they speak to make sure their words are not misunderstood. Consider the following real-life examples of announcements that have appeared in various church bulletins. Whoever wrote the announcements didn't think through the words they were using and the announcements ended up leaving the wrong impression. Get ready to laugh!

If any of the members of the congregation have children and don't know it, there is a nursery downstairs.

This week we invite any member of the congregation who enjoys sinning to join the choir.

This being Easter Sunday, we will ask Mrs. Lewis to come forward and lay an egg on the altar.

"Weight Watchers" will meet at 7 p.m. in the church hall. Please use large double door at the side entrance.

Next Sunday a special collection will be taken to defray the cost of the new carpet. All those wishing to do something on the new carpet will come forward and do so.

Bertha Belch, a missionary from Africa will be speaking tonight at Calvary Memorial Church in Racine. Come tonight and hear Bertha Belch all the way from Africa.

Ladies, don't forget the rummage sale. It's a chance to get rid of those things not worth keeping around the house. Don't forget your husbands.

Even though these announcements are funny, they remind us of how easy it is to leave the wrong impression when we are careless with our words. And I'm betting that the churches who made the mistakes in the announcements, sure wish they had taken a few more minutes to ponder their words before putting them in print!

This Monday we will be holding a "Bean Supper" in the church hall. Music will follow.

JUST BETWEEN US

1. In verses 8, 14, and 19, what two words (one is the same in two of the verses) show up that remind you of a leaky faucet?

2. How can the "babbling of a fool" (vs. 14) invite trouble? Can you think of a situation involving you or one of your friends where this happened? If yes, describe it but don't use any names!

3. In verse 19, what does it say the solution is for babbling, chattering, or using too many words?

4. After reading the above verses in Proverbs 10, do you have a better understanding of why our words should be considered carefully?

PSSST, GOD!

If gossip is a problem for you, take a minute and ask God to help you "turn off the flow." Pray He will give you the strength to hold your tongue the next time you are tempted to gossip or pass along gossip you heard from someone else.

SEARCHIN' THE WORD

Find the words you have learned from the Proverbial Dictionary!

Adultery	Foolishness	Prudence
Discretion	Humility	Righteous
Ensnared	Insight	Trust
Fear of the Lord	Instruction	Understanding
Folly	Integrity	Upright
Fool	Knowledge	Wisdom
	Pride	Wise

Proverbs 11

Proverbs 11:17 Your own soul is nourished when you are kind, but you destroy yourself when you are cruel.

recently did a survey where I asked girls between the ages of 8 to 12 to tell me about a time when another girl was really mean to them. One of the girls who answered the questions on the survey is named Shelby and she's 11 years old. She described an extremely hurtful event where she was training for her very first horse show. She was riding her pony at the stables and a girl who practiced at the same time began to taunt her and say some really mean things to Shelby. She teased Shelby and said, "Your horse will never be show material." This became a pattern and every time Shelby went to the stables to ride, the girl was ready with new ammunition. She would also talk behind Shelby's back to the other girls and tell them that Shelby's family didn't have much money and that she probably wouldn't be able to afford to show her horse much longer. She would brag to the other girls about how much longer she had been riding horses than Shelby and even told Shelby that she would "kick her rear end" if they showed their horses at the same show. She actually used a very bad word in the place of "rear end."

Shelby went ahead and told her mother and her mother encouraged her to do her best to try to ignore the mean girl's comments and not allow her to stand in the way of her goal. Shelby said she cried at first because all she wanted to do was fit in and have a good time. Her mom encouraged her to find new friends to ride with and Shelby did just that. And guess what happened? Shelby won a Grand Champion ribbon with her pony! Sometimes she still sees the mean girl at the stables, but Shelby said, "I am always nice and kind to her. It makes me feel good to be nice to other people." Isn't that amazing?!

When I read Proverbs 11:17, I thought of Shelby and that mean girl at the stables. Shelby "nourished her own soul" by being kind. Just like a plant needs water (nourishment) to grow and be healthy, being kind to others can be like watering our souls, so they will be healthy. The mean girl, on the other hand, was only hurting herself by being mean. She thought she was hurting Shelby when she dished out her cruel comments, but in the end her plan backfired. She may not realize it, but little by little, she is destroying her own soul with every cruel remark she makes. In other words, she's really hurting herself by being mean! The next time someone is mean to you, remember Shelby's story. It's hard to hold your head up high and be kind when someone is mean to you, but in doing so you are nourishing your very own soul!

JUST BETWEEN US

1. Can you think of a time when someone was mean to you? Describe what happened. (Remember not to use names if you are doing this as a group and other girls may know who you are talking about.)

2. How did you react to situation? Did you tell your mother?

JUST BETWEEN US

(continued)

3. Were you able to be kind to the person instead of being mean back? (Remember, being kind doesn't always mean remaining friends!)

4. The next time you encounter (come across) someone who is being mean, what will you remember about Proverbs 11:17? You may not be able to change the situation, but you can control how you respond. Do you think you'll respond by being mean back to the person? Or do you think you'll respond by being kind and ignoring the person as much as possible? If you choose to be kind, what is the prize?

PSSST, GOD!

Pray and ask God to show you if you have been behaving like a mean girl. There might be someone you need to apologize to in an effort to make things right. Now pray for any girls who come to mind who have been behaving like mean girls. Ask God to change their hearts and help them see how serious He is about the sins above.

The LORD abhors dishonest scales, but accurate weights are his delight. (Proverbs 11:1 NIV)

Say WHAT?

In Bible times merchants (sellers) would set up in the marketplace to sell their goods to the townspeople. They didn't have "grocery stores," so the marketplace was like their Walmart! To figure out how much to charge a customer for something like grain (to make bread), the seller would have to weigh it first. Some sellers, who weren't honest, would use a scale that didn't measure the true weight, and it would say that the grain was heavier than it actually was. The customer would pay for a pound, but only get ¾ of a pound.

It would be like weighing yourself on your bathroom scale at home that is broken. Maybe it is set to where it starts at five pounds instead of zero before you ever step up on the scale. When the number comes up, it's going to be five pounds heavier than you actually are. It's not hard to figure out that this verse above is talking about honesty. The Lord abhors (hates) dishonesty but delights in accurate weights. It's true: honesty IS the best policy!

When you think of pigs, what's the first thing that comes to your mind? Maybe your initial thought is that pigs are cute, but I bet close behind is that they're dirty and filthy and like to slosh around in mud baths! So, what on earth does a pig have to do with gold rings? In Bible times gold rings were meant to make a woman appear more beautiful.

> Like a gold ring in a pig's snout is a beautiful woman who shows no discretion. (Proverbs 11:22 NIV)

Nothing. That's exactly the point here! A filthy, smelly pig with a beautiful gold ring in his snout would look ridiculous! It just doesn't go together. It would be like putting OJ instead of milk in your cereal, or even worse, dipping your Oreos into a jar of pickle juice! Just like pigs and golden rings don't go together; neither does a beautiful woman without morals or good sense. The gold ring is valuable, but it seems like a big waste if a woman without good sense wears one. Just like the delicious taste of an Oreo is ruined if dipped in pickle juice, a woman's outer beauty is spoiled by her unwise actions. Beauty is more than skin deep—what you see on the outside is not always what you get on the inside!

> A gentle answer turns away wrath, but a harsh word stirs up anger. (Proverbs 15:1 NIV)

If you have a little brother, or have ever observed some of the boys' actions in your grade, then you know that boys seem to look for trouble! One thing that seems to be awfully tempting is for boys to pass by an ant-hill and leave it alone. It's almost like they're wired somewhere inside themselves to find a stick when they see an anthill and declare war on it. And when that happens, run for the hills or you may find yourself covered in angry, homeless ants. Those little suckers don't care who they bite, so good luck if you're standing anywhere nearby! Trust me, they aren't going to come out and take the time to try to figure out who the villain was that destroyed their anthill apartments! It's payback time!

The verse above talks about how we can handle people who speak to us in an angry or mean tone of voice. It says that the wisest action we can take is to reply with a gentle, calm answer or tone of voice. Think about it. Imagine you were frustrated or angry with someone (Mom maybe?), and you replied to her with a loud, angry voice. If she continues to reply back to you in a gentle tone of voice (before she sends you to your room!), it would be hard to continue to reply back to her in anger.

The same is true for you. If someone says something to you in an angry tone of voice, reply with a gentle, calm answer. You might have to pause, take a deep breath, and count to ten (silently in your head or they might think you're a bit crazy!) before you reply. Replying to anger with a gentle tone takes a lot of self-control, because our natural, sinful reaction is to want to be angry right back at the person. Maybe it will help if you picture that person as the Queen Ant sitting on top of the anthill mound. Are you going to poke back?

Proverbs 12

Proverbs 12:11 Hard work means prosperity; only fools idle away their time.

Proverbs 12:24 Work hard and become a leader; be lazy and become a slave.

I remember a time in high school where I witnessed the reward for hard work . . . only, it was someone else's hard work! It was my senior year and I was sitting in the bleachers of the gym with my friends during the awards ceremony at the end of the year. I was part of the "popular crowd" and our group was made up of students who had grown used to getting a lot of attention over the years. We were the cheerleaders, football players, drill team girls, and other athletes who pretty much ruled the school. Until awards day, that is . . . As we sat in the bleachers in our little clique of popular people, we watched as students we'd hardly known accept one award after another. They were awarded scholarships to colleges, certificates for perfect math scores, recognition for their leadership in the academic clubs, and the list went on and on. One by one, as their names were called, they would make their way to the front of the gym, serenaded by a round of celebratory applause.

All the while, those of us in the "popular crowd" sat and fidgeted. For the first time the attention was on the students who deserved to be honored and recognized for their hard work and true achievement. I can't speak for the other students in my group, but I know I was feeling a bit of jealousy and more importantly, regret. Regret that I hadn't tried harder or recognized the investment that comes from pouring yourself into things that truly matter. While I was busy keeping up with all the image-maintenance issues that come with the territory of being popular, these students were busy studying and investing in their future success. Funny, there wasn't an award given to the person who had managed to have the coolest clothes or a scholarship given to the person who was voted "Class Favorite." There were no certificates handed out for being pretty or handsome. Zippo. Nada. Zilch.

I'm not saying that being smart, going to good colleges, and getting good jobs will lead to future happiness. Only a life lived centered around Christ will offer the stability and happiness our hearts crave. But I do think there are more important things to worry about at your age than being popular. If you invest in things that matter, you will reap a reward. Hard work always pays off.

1. If you look up the word *prosperity* in the dictionary, you will find words like: "advance or gain in anything good or desirable; good fortune; success." In verse 11, what brings "prosperity"?

2. The last part of verse 11 says, "only fools idle away their time." What do you think that means? (Hint: You might need to look up the word *idle* if you don't know what it means.)

3. For the people who "idle away their time," what does verse 24 say might happen to them?

4. Can you think of a time in your life where you worked really hard for something and it paid off? If so, what was it and what was the award?

JUST BETWEEN US

PSSST, GOD!

Pray and ask God to help you make the most of your time and invest it in things that really matter. Most importantly, ask Him to help you invest time in getting to know Him and the plan and purpose He has for your life.

Look up the verses below and rewrite them to change the *LIES* back into **Wise** Bible verses!

LIE: Trusting in our riches (wealth/money) will make us happy. (Proverbs 11:28)

to Wise: _____

LIE: Be friends with everyone, including those headed for trouble! (Proverbs 12:26)

to Wise: _____

LIE: If you're disciplined, just ignore it. (Proverbs 13:18)

to Wise: _____

LIE: The Lord hears the prayers of the wicked. (Proverbs 15:29)

to Wise: _____

LIE: Being patient is foolish, but displaying a quick temper shows understanding (Proverbs 14:29)

to Wise: _____

LIE: The way of righteousness is death. (Proverbs 12:28)

to Wise: _____

LIE: Being mean gains respect. (Proverbs 11:16)

to Wise: _____

LIE: The Lord can't watch over everyone at the same time. (Proverbs 15:3)

to Wise: _____

Proverbs 13

When I was in middle school, I joined the track team. I was pretty fast in the short distance races and would generally take home a first, second, or third place ribbon. I'm not sure if they still give out ribbons at track meets, but I always enjoyed getting the first place blue ribbons and tacking them on my bulletin board at home. I had a great coach who really liked me and encouraged me as a runner. One day at practice she announced that I would be running in a long distance, half-mile race at the upcoming track meet. I had never run long distance before, but I felt pretty sure I could do it. I had two weeks to get in shape and my coach took the time to give me some great training tips.

One bit of advice my coach gave me was to resist the urge to run fast in the first lap. She said it was more important to find a good medium pace and save my energy for when I really needed it in the final lap. She had me practice with some of the other girls who ran long distance and I did a pretty good job of keeping up with their pace for the first lap. On the second and final lap, I was usually behind, but by the end of the two weeks, I was beginning to get the hang of it and finish somewhere in the middle of the pack.

and the first place winner is . . .

Proverbs 13:10 Pride leads to arguments; those who take advice are wise.

Proverbs 13:13 People who despise advice will find themselves in trouble; those who respect it will succeed.

Proverbs 13:14 The advice of the wise is like a life-giving fountain; those who accept it avoid the snares of death.

The day of the track meet came and when they announced the half-mile race, I lined up with the rest of the contestants in the blocks. It's always nerve-racking when you're waiting for the gun to sound after the familiar, "Runners to your mark . . . get set . . . go! When the gun went off signaling the start of the race, I left the blocks at full-speed. I don't know what came over me, but I kept up my fast pace, knowing that I was going against the advice and training of my coach. It just felt good to be so far ahead of the pack and I really thought I could keep up the pace and win the race. Besides, I wanted another blue ribbon to tack on my bulletin board!

Well, you probably know what happened next. By the second lap I was beginning to lose energy just as the other girls were gaining on me. One by one each girl passed me while I struggled to keep up. By the time I stumbled awkwardly across the finish line, I was far behind the other girls and bent over with a cramp in my side and a look of embarrassment on my face. I came in dead last. No ribbon to tack onto my bulletin board after that race!

I'll never forget my coach's look of disappointment when I walked over to her after the race. All she said was, "Vicki, you just discovered why it's important to listen to your coach when you're training for a race. I bet you won't make that mistake again." And you can bet that I didn't! The next time my coach put me in a long distance race, I followed her advice to a tee. I finished somewhere in the middle of the pack, but I didn't care. Anything was better than coming in dead last and having everyone in the stands staring at me with a look of pity!

I came in dead last . . . no ribbon to tack onto my bulletin board!

JUST BETWEEN US

1. Read Proverbs 13:13. How did my story relate to the verse?

2. Can you think of a time where you were given good advice and it paid off? What was it?

3. Can you think of a time where you were given good advice and you didn't follow it? What happened?

4. Can you think of advice that parents often give to help their children avoid the "snares of death"? (Ex: "Look both ways before crossing the street"; "Don't talk to strangers.")

People who despise advice will find themselves in trouble; those who respect it will succeed. Proverbs 13:13

PSSST, GOD!

Take a minute and thank God for the advice He gives in His Word. Also thank Him for sending others to give you good advice. Ask Him to help you put aside your pride the next time you are given good advice and follow it.

IN THIS CORNER
DILIGENCE vs LAZINESS

Proverbs talks often about the quality of being a hard worker. Genesis 2:2 says, *"By the seventh day, God completed His work that He had done, and He rested on the seventh day from all His work that He had done."* Did you know that work is actually something God gave us to enjoy with Him? He gave Adam and Eve an important job right from the beginning of creation. Genesis 2:15 says, *"The LORD God took the man and placed him in the garden of Eden to work it and watch over it."* It is pretty clear that God honors work and He considers it a blessing and godly virtue! Let's see how you approach work.

Rate yourself on a scale of 1-10 based on how you typically act. The closer to 1 you circle, the closer you typically behave to the statement on the left and vice versa. Remember, nobody's perfect, so don't be embarrassed to find you have room to improve in some areas.

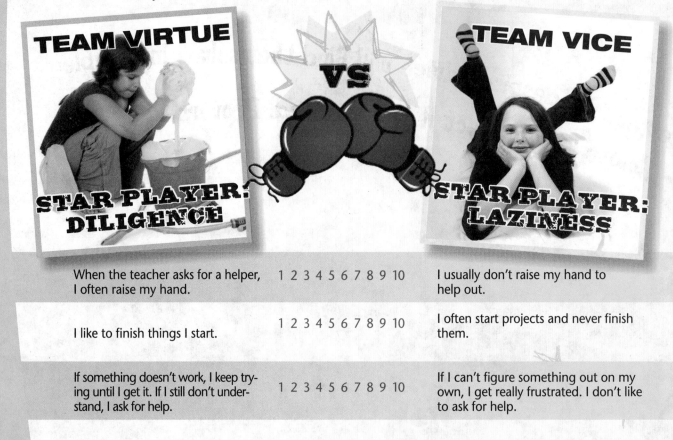

TEAM VIRTUE VS TEAM VICE

STAR PLAYER: DILIGENCE

STAR PLAYER: LAZINESS

When the teacher asks for a helper, I often raise my hand.	1 2 3 4 5 6 7 8 9 10	I usually don't raise my hand to help out.
I like to finish things I start.	1 2 3 4 5 6 7 8 9 10	I often start projects and never finish them.
If something doesn't work, I keep trying until I get it. If I still don't understand, I ask for help.	1 2 3 4 5 6 7 8 9 10	If I can't figure something out on my own, I get really frustrated. I don't like to ask for help.
I usually do my homework without being told.	1 2 3 4 5 6 7 8 9 10	I wait until someone tells me I have to do homework to start on it.
If I commit, I stick to it, even if it's not something I enjoy.	1 2 3 4 5 6 7 8 9 10	I usually ask if I can quit sports or lessons if I end up not liking them.

In group projects I do my share of work.	1 2 3 4 5 6 7 8 9 10	I try to pick the job that has the least amount of work in group projects.
I do chores without complaining.	1 2 3 4 5 6 7 8 9 10	I groan when I'm asked to do chores.
I start working on assignments pretty quickly after they are assigned.	1 2 3 4 5 6 7 8 9 10	I wait until the very last minute to get started on assignments.
I try to get exercise weekly through sports or other activities.	1 2 3 4 5 6 7 8 9 10	I don't exercise much. I'm pretty much a couch potato.
When helping around the house, I concentrate on getting the job done.	1 2 3 4 5 6 7 8 9 10	When helping out around the house, I am easily distracted.

Now, total up the numbers you circled to see what corner you're in! How did you do?

KNOCKOUT!

If you scored between 10 and 39, you are a hard working girl! You see the value of taking responsibility for your health, your school work, and helping around the house. You understand that you play a very important role at home and in class! Good job. You have chosen wisely! Keep it up, and work to improve in any areas where you show a weakness.

DANCING AROUND THE RING

If you scored between 40 and 70, you can go either way. Sometimes you are diligent in what you do, but other times you can slip into patterns of laziness. You have some things you may need to work on, but don't be discouraged. Most of us can relate to being in the middle. I know it's hard to fight laziness (from a fellow struggler), but it is worth it! Start working on the areas where you scored a 7 or higher.

DOWN FOR THE COUNT!

If you scored between 71 and 100, you have a tendency to take the easy way out and choose laziness over diligence. Perhaps you don't yet see the unique role you play in your class and family when you step up to the plate and do your part. It might take a while, but take one of the "vices" on page 62 where you scored a 9 or 10 and work on it this week. Then, pick another one for next week. Remember: diligence means that you are consistently working hard, so this will be a good start!

Proverbs 14

Proverbs 14:15 Only simpletons believe everything they are told! The prudent carefully consider their steps.

Proverbs 14:16 The wise are cautious and avoid danger; fools plunge ahead with great confidence.

Sleep on it

If you walked into my office, you would find a post-it note on my computer monitor that says, "sleep on it." Sometimes I get stressful phone calls or e-mails where it would be easy to immediately respond without thinking through the consequences. I learned this little "sleep on it" trick from my coworkers who started the fad of putting the post-it note on their monitors to help remind them to think things through for at least a night before making a big decision or responding to a difficult situation.

My post-it note saved me one time when I received a difficult call from a lady who wanted to come to one of my events. She left an angry voice mail message saying that when she went to register for the event online, she discovered it was already sold-out. I was super mad when I heard her message because I couldn't understand why she was calling and blaming us for the fact that she didn't register for the event in time!! However, I practiced the post-it note wisdom and decided to "sleep on it" before calling her back. The next day she ended up leaving another message before I could get around to calling her back, and this time she apologized for her attitude on the day before! Good thing I "slept on it" and didn't call her back right away.

Carefully consider your steps

Like Proverbs 14:15–16 says, "The prudent carefully consider their steps" while "fools plunge ahead." If you look the word *prudent* up in the dictionary, you might find a definition that says something like: "wise, careful, exercising good judgment." God wants us to be careful when it comes to making decisions. I remember when I was in 5th grade and a bunch of my friends were signing up to play soccer. I was big into gymnastics and I really enjoyed it. However, I wanted to do what my friends were doing, so I begged my mom to let me sign up for the soccer team. She tried to discourage me from doing it since I was already participating in gymnastics, but I wouldn't listen. I signed up for the team, bought the uniform and a brand new pair of cleats, and headed off to practice. After one practice I decided I absolutely hated playing soccer, but my mom made me keep my commitment. I got so tired trying to play two sports and dreaded every soccer practice and game. I sat on the sidelines during most of the games anyway, since I wasn't all that good. If I had taken the time to "consider my steps" and really think the decision through, I would have made a wiser choice.

As you get older, many of the decisions you will face will be more serious than a decision about whether or not to play on a sports team. Maybe you'll say "yes" to dating too soon or cave into peer pressure and drink alcohol at a party. Maybe you'll react to a rumor and lash out in anger before you have all the facts. If you get into the habit of "carefully considering your steps," chances are, you'll be more likely to keep a cool head when the big decisions come down the pipe in the years to come.

Most importantly, when you think something through or "sleep on it," you have time to run it past God, pray about it, and get His opinion. And in the end, that's the only opinion that really matters.

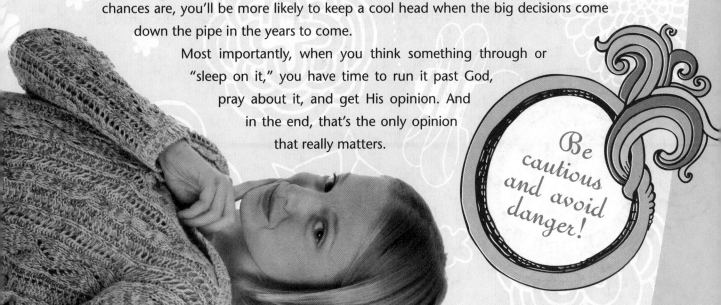

Be cautious and avoid danger!

JUST BETWEEN US

1. Can you think of a time when you faced a difficult decision? Did you rush into making the decision or take some time to "consider your steps carefully"?

2. Can you think of a situation where you or someone you know rushed into making a decision (plunged ahead) and things didn't work out very well? What was it?

3. When was the last time you took the time to pray about a situation and ask God to help you make a decision? What was it?

4. In verse 16, what is the reward for when the "wise are cautious"?

PSSST, GOD!

Are you facing a decision right now? If so, take a minute to pray and talk to God about it. Ask Him to help you make the right choice and show you the path He wants you to take.

Quiz

R U a gossip queen?

Pssst, want to know a secret?

Gossip is a big problem. Well, I guess that's not really a secret and you probably knew that already. In fact, chances are you've experienced the negative effects of gossip by now. Gossip can be defined many ways. It includes: sharing secrets/stories that aren't yours to tell, imagining things about a person without having the facts and sharing it with others, starting rumors, and joining in with someone else who is talking about another person.

The worst part about gossip is that it can destroy friendships. Thankfully there is a cure for gossip—you! God can give you the strength to stop, but you have to first admit you have a problem and then ask for His help. Take the quiz on the next two pages to see how you measure up against gossip!

Friends tell friends everything, right?

1. When your teacher was handing back the tests, you accidentally saw Brady's test grade and let's just say, it wasn't good. Surprisingly you ended up doing pretty well. Later that day your friends begin talking about how hard the test was and the grades they got.
You . . .

A) Agree with them and tell them what you made.

B) Agree with them, and tell them that you saw Brady's score and he got a D!

2. You usually sit with the same group of friends at lunch and notice that Kaitlyn hasn't really been eating her lunch the past few days. You . . .

A) Keep quiet, and ask Kaitlyn later when you're in private if everything is OK.

B) When Kaitlyn leaves the table, you ask your friends if they might think she has an eating disorder.

3. At cheerleading practice Michelle shows up very late. She was pulled out of class earlier in the day and sent to the principal's office. You are sure there's a juicy story behind it. You . . .

A) Ask her after practice if everything is OK. You're worried about her.

B) Glance at your friends and talk afterward about all the possible reasons she could have been in trouble.

4. Walking down the hallway, you see one of your classmates trip and fall flat on his face, books flying everywhere! He wasn't hurt and brushed it off, but you thought it was hilarious. You walk back to class and sit down next to your friend. Dying to tell her, you . . .

A) Resist the temptation and talk about something else to take your mind off of it.

B) Cover your muffled laugh with your hand and immediately begin to spill out the story to your friend.

5. In the bathroom you overhear Jennifer and Emily talking about how they think Hayden is the cutest boy in school. You return to class and sit next to your very best friend. You . . .

A) Say nothing because you wouldn't want someone to share that information about you.

B) Pass a note to your friend detailing

the conversation you just overheard. Friends tell friends everything, right?

6. Nicole tells you that her parents are getting a divorce. It's kind of shocking because Nicole's mom is very involved as a volunteer at your school and her dad is a teacher there. The next time Nicole's mom volunteers in your class, you . . .

A) Remember what Nicole said, and make a mental note to ask Nicole later how she's doing.

B) Lean over to your friend Maddie and whisper, "Did you hear that Nicole's mom is getting a divorce?"

7. Over the weekend you go to a movie with your friend Hannah. While at the movie theater, you see one of your church friends walking out of an R-rated movie. You . . .

A) Say nothing and do nothing. You might ask her about it later, but you'll pray about it first.

B) Immediately text your best friend "Remind me to tell you something about Casey later!"

8. A girl in your grade, Rachel, suddenly transfers to another school. You and your friends are talking about why she left and there's a rumor that she did something really bad. You . . .

A) Say, "We don't know what happened and we shouldn't be talking about it." and immediately change the subject.

B) Say, "Ooohhh. I bet you're right. She's kinda strange."

How did U score?

MYOB: Mind your own business!

Did you score mostly A's? If so, you understand the benefits of staying out of things that don't concern you! You keep information to yourself, even if you are dying to tell someone. You value being someone who does not participate in gossip and understand the negative effects it can have on friendships and your own reputation. Even though things might sometimes slip out, you understand that it's not right. Keep a close watch when you start conversations with "Guess what I heard?" or "Did you hear . . . ?" Keep it up, and try to catch yourself when you're tempted to give into the gossip bug!

DM: Drama Mama

Did you score mostly B's? If so, you are a Drama Mama! If there is drama going on, you usually have a major part in the show! Even though you try hard, you just can't resist asking questions to find out information about others. And, sometimes you struggle with telling news or information that just isn't yours to tell. Take charge, Drama Mama! You can control your tongue by not participating in gossip, no matter how tempting the situation is. Walk away from situations where you're listening to gossip, and practice holding your tongue by not sharing everything with your friends, even your BFF. In the end you'll develop healthy friendships that won't be torn apart by gossip. And remember, if you're hanging around girls who gossip about others all the time, there's a good chance they also gossip about you when you're not around! True friends don't share gossip. Period!

Proverbs 15

Proverbs 15:14 A wise person is hungry for truth, while the fool feeds on trash.

If you grew up going to church, you probably remember singing this song:

O be careful little eyes what you see
O be careful little eyes what you see
There's a Father up above
And He's looking down in love
So, be careful little eyes what you see

O be careful little ears what you hear
O be careful little ears what you hear
There's a Father up above
And He's looking down in love
So, be careful little ears what you hear

The idea behind the song is that the things we see and hear will impact the way we behave. Just as eating too much junk food is bad for your heart, the same is true for some of the junk we watch on TV, some of the songs we listen to, some of the movies we watch, and even some of the friends we hang out with who may be bad influences.

Proverbs 15:14 tells us that a wise person is hungry for truth, while the fool feeds on trash. One mother, sitting next to me on an airplane on a recent trip home, told me a story about her six-year-old daughter who had just gotten in trouble for singing the chorus to her favorite song while at recess. The song was a popular song that was playing often on the pop radio station, but the words were pure trash. The mother shared that she had never thought it was a big deal to let her daughter listen to that radio station until now. It was a wake-up call for her to change the station!

The story above is a great example of how what we hear can affect what we say or do. You might have heard the saying before, "Garbage in, garbage out."

That's why God tells us that it's important to "be careful" about what we take in because it will influence our behavior. If we listen to too much trash talk, it's only a matter of time before we are talking trashy. If we watch too much trash TV, we will eventually begin to think it's normal to imitate what we see. If we hang out with friends who use bad language, after awhile we will sound just like them. Be careful little eyes and little ears what you see and hear. The Father up above is looking down in love, so make Him proud!

JUST BETWEEN US

1. Can you think of an example of something you may have seen or heard that was not something God would want you to see or hear? If so, what was it?

2. Do you know anyone who makes it a habit to listen to trashy music or watch trashy shows? Have you noticed any ways that it has affected their behavior?

3. Have you ever been in a situation where someone has tempted you to watch or listen to something trashy? If yes, how did you react?

4. Let's pretend that you are at a party and your friends put a DVD in that you know your parents wouldn't approve of. Write down what you might say to your friends in that situation.

5. What are some ways you can feed on God's truth instead?

Be HUNGRY for the Truth!

PSSST, GOD!

Pray and ask God to help you recognize when you come in contact with something that is inappropriate. Ask Him to give you the strength to say "no" to harmful influences.

PROVERBS CROSSWORD PUZZLE

Use the Proverbs Scripture references to complete this crossword puzzle. See if you can answer it first, without looking it up to test your knowledge of Proverbs!

Across:

3 This type of man is wise in his own eyes (*Proverbs 28:11*)

5 The body part that is mentioned as a warning against dishonesty (*Proverbs 4:24*)

8 Our reaction to wisdom (*Proverbs 2:2*)

11 The two things your should write on the tablet of your heart (*Proverbs 3:3*)

14 What the Lord will be in times of sudden disaster (*Proverbs 3:25–26*)

15 Words spoken at the right time are like this "golden" fruit (*Proverbs 25:11*)

17 Part of the eye we are to protect, as we protect the wise teachings of the Bible (*Proverbs 7:2*)

19 This type of person shows great understanding (*Proverbs 14:29*)

20 This is what a gossip reveals (*Proverbs 20:19*)

22 The other thing fools despise (*Proverbs 1:7*)

24 What wisdom is more profitable than (*Proverbs 3:14*)

25 The insect we are to observe to become wise (*Proverbs 6:6*)

26 One thing fools despise (*Proverbs 1:7*)

27 Who is separated by gossip? (*Proverbs 17:9*)

28 What the name of the Lord is to those who run to it (*Proverbs 18:10*)

Down:

1 Men can "sharpen" each other, just like this metal does (*Proverbs 27:17*)

2 This animal is prepared for battle, but victory comes from the Lord. (*Proverbs 21:31*)

4 What we are to guard above all else (*Proverbs 4:23*)

6 What we shouldn't do (*Proverbs 25:6*)

7 What the Lord weighs (examines), regardless of what seems right to us (*Proverbs 16:2*)

9 The body part that contains both the power of life and death (*Proverbs 18:21*)

10 This is to be chosen over wealth (*Proverbs 22:1*)

12 What we are not supposed to rely upon (*Proverbs 3:5*)

13 The Lord determines these for men (*Proverbs 20:24*)

14 What wise people listen to (*Proverbs 12:15*)

16 This type of answer turns away anger (*Proverbs 15:1*)

18 The words of God are described this way (*Proverbs 30:5*)

21 Number of pillars in the house of wisdom (*Proverbs 9:1*)

23 Without this, people will fall (*Proverbs 11:14*)

Need help? Choose from these words:

apple	brag	seven	tongue
friends	good name	pupil	love and faithfulness
pure	secrets	steps	silver
knowledge	tower	listen	guidance
rich	motives	ant	counsel
iron	patient	mouth	understanding
			gentle
			horse
			confidence
			heart
			wisdom

Words satisfy the soul . . .

Beginning a quarrel is like opening a floodgate . . .

Proverbs 16-20

A truly wise person uses few words.

We can make our plans, but the LORD determines our steps.

Proverbs 16

Proverbs 16:9 We can make our plans, but the LORD determines our steps.

Proverbs 16:33 We may throw the dice, but the LORD determines how they fall.

I know that getting married is probably not at the top of your to-do list right now, but when you get older, you'll probably put some thought into the kind of guy you'll marry. Some girls even make a list of the qualities they hope their future husband will have. In fact, when my daughter was eight years old, she wrote a note to me in the front of my Bible during church one Sunday. It said this:

We had talked before about the importance of Christians only marrying fellow Christians, but I guess she threw in the other two qualities as bonus features. She's not married, so I can't tell you if she will stick to her plans. I can tell you that she's in college now and she didn't end up going to The University of Texas! Plans can change, I suppose.

> Mom, someday I'm
> going to marry a guy who:
> a. has blue eyes
> b. is a Longhorn fan.
>   (the University of Texas)
> c. Is a Christian

What about you? Do you have hopes and dreams for the future? Most everyone does. Maybe you've thought about what you want to be when you grow up or what kind of house you want to live in. Maybe you've dreamed about traveling around the world and seeing the sights. Or maybe you've even thought about the kind of guy you hope to marry and started your list.

It's great to make plans, but it's important that we give God room to work and make changes if necessary. I love how Proverbs 16:33 says, "We may throw the dice, but the LORD determines how they fall." You've probably played a board game before and thrown dice as part of the game. And you know that there's nothing you can do to control what numbers come up on the dice. For example, even if my daughter marries a guy who's a Christian, has blue eyes, and is a Longhorn fan, does that mean that they'll live happily ever after? Not necessarily.

Making plans is not a bad idea. However, in the end, God always has the final say. He wants us to trust Him no matter what comes up on the dice.

Trust GOD no matter what!

JUST BETWEEN US

1. Have you made any plans for the future? If so, share an example.

2. In the past, have you ever made plans and then been disappointed that your plans didn't work out as you had hoped? What happened?

3. It's hard to understand when things happen that are outside of our "plans." Is God still in control?

4. God wants us to trust Him in all areas of our lives. Can you trust Him?

PSSST, GOD!

Take a minute to pray. Ask God to help you trust Him with the future. If you like to make plans, get in the habit of giving your plans over to the Lord by telling Him, "Your will be done."

Answers to Proverbs crossword puzzle on page 72

Say WHAT?

Better to meet a bear robbed of her cubs than a fool in his folly. (Proverbs 17:12 NIV)

BACK OFF!

Have you ever seen a mama bear with her cubs? Or for that matter, have you been around any animal mama with new babies? They are suspicious of anyone who comes near and super-protective. If you even try to get close, the mama feels threatened and usually defends her babies (just like Mom did with you!). I remember a time when I tried to get near a new litter of puppies to pet them, and the mama dog bit me on the ankle!

Now, stop for a minute and imagine what a mama bear might do if someone robbed her of her cubs and took them away from her. If she catches the thief, she'd probably do a lot more than bite his ankle! The verse above tells us that being around mama bear who was just robbed of her cubs is BETTER than hanging around a fool who makes foolish decisions! Whoa! Just as it would be dangerous to be around a mama bear that has been robbed of her cubs, the same is often true for fools who constantly make foolish choices. Stay away or you might find yourself in a beary (sorry, I couldn't resist!) dangerous situation.

Did you know that the tongue is one of the strongest muscles in our body? Yep, that's right. That weird, reddish, gummy thing in your mouth just happens to be incredibly strong! We rely on our tongues for a lot: chewing, swallowing, tasting, and even speaking! Have you ever tried to speak without using your tongue? Try it by holding your tongue with your fingers. Now, reread this last paragraph out loud. Not easy, huh?

Just as our tongues can be powerful muscles to help us when we eat, they can also be powerful muscles when it comes to our speech. The words we choose can bring a smile to someone's face or . . . a frown. Sometimes, our words can even hurt others and cause tears. Chances are you've cried before over something cruel or mean someone has said to you, so you know what I'm talking about. But, have you ever been the one to say something cruel and mean?

James 3:5 tells us our words make a difference. Just like a small spark can create a huge forest fire, so too, our small tongues can create a huge mess. This verse in Proverbs says that life and death are in the power of the tongue! An encouraging word can breathe life into someone having a bad day, just as a harsh word can crush someone's spirit. How are you using your tongue? Does it bring life or death to others? The choice is yours.

The tongue has the power of life and death, and those who love it will eat its fruit (Proverbs 18:21 NIV)

Likewise the tongue is a small part of the body, but it makes great boasts. Consider what a great forest is set on fire by a small spark. (James 3:5 NIV)

It is not good to have zeal without knowledge, nor to be hasty and miss the way. (Proverbs 19:2 NIV)

If you look up the word *zeal* in the dictionary, you might find words like: "passion" or "devotion." Maybe you are "passionately devoted" to a favorite TV show or your pet gerbil, Rocky. Maybe you are "passionately devoted" to making a 100 on the upcoming spelling test. But what if you didn't study for the test or feed your gerbil? You can have passion about making a good grade on the test or loving good ol' Rocky the gerbil, but if you don't practice what you preach, you may end up with an "F" on your paper and a very hungry gerbil on your hands!

If you look up *hasty* in the dictionary, you might find words like: "speedy," "quick" or "hurried." The verse above reminds us that it's not good to have zeal (passionate devotion) or to be hasty (speedy, quick) without applying knowledge (duh, our brains!). In other words, it's best to "think before you speak" and "look before you leap."

Proverbs 17

Proverbs 17:9 Disregarding another person's faults preserves love; telling about them separates close friends.

Proverbs 17:14 Beginning a quarrel is like opening a floodgate, so drop the matter before a dispute breaks out.

Proverbs 17:19 Anyone who loves to quarrel loves sin; anyone who speaks boastfully invites disaster.

Proverbs 17:27 A truly wise person uses few words; a person with understanding is even-tempered.

If there had been a "Girl Drama Club" in middle school and high school, I would have been the president. If there was a rumor to spread or a fight to start, I was usually somewhere in the middle of it. In the group of girls I hung out with, one of my friends hated drama. If we were all hanging out together and trying to decide on pepperoni or cheese pizza, Karen would say, *"I don't care. It doesn't matter to me."* If we were taking a vote on whether to go swimming or watch a movie, she would say, *"I don't care. It doesn't matter to me."*

There were five of us who hung out together, so it was super-irritating if whatever we were voting on boiled down to a split 2/2 tie. Sometimes, when that happened, an argument would break out and we would all turn to Karen and beg her to cast her vote. Of course, her answer was always, *"I don't care. It doesn't matter to me."* After awhile we got so irritated with her that we nicknamed her, "Little Miss It-Doesn't-Matter" since she would never take a side.

Now, as I look back, I wish I had been the one to be nicknamed "Little Miss It-Doesn't-Matter." Proverbs 17:27 reminds us that "A truly wise person uses few words; a person with understanding is even-tempered." It turns out Karen was the only wise one in our bunch when it came to arguing and taking sides! Maybe we should all practice saying, *"I don't care. It doesn't matter to me"* when we find ourselves smack-dab in the middle of an argument!

JUST BETWEEN US

1. How might practicing the first part of Proverbs 17:19 help you stay out of arguments with friends?

2. Proverbs 17:14 tells us to "drop the matter before a dispute breaks out." Are you generally one to "drop the matter" or "keep it going"?

3. Can you think of a time where a fight broke out among you and your friends because you couldn't all agree on something? If so, what was it?

4. How might you have changed your response (if at all) to the situation mentioned earlier after reading the verses above?

Pray and ask God to help you be a peacemaker when arguments break out. Ask Him for the strength to drop the matter before a dispute breaks out and to use few words in an effort to be more even-tempered.

LIES to WISE

Look up the verses below and rewrite them to change the **LIES** back into **Wise** Bible verses!

LIE: *Gold and silver are way better than wisdom and understanding. (Proverbs 16:16)*

to Wise: _____

LIE: *When someone wrongs us, we should pay them back. (Proverbs 20:22)*

to Wise: _____

LIE: *Gossip strengthens friendships. (Proverbs 16:28)*

to Wise: _____

LIE: *A friend sometimes loves you. (Proverbs 17:17)*

to Wise: _____

LIE: *Man determines his own steps. (Proverbs 16:9)*

to Wise: _____

LIE: *It's wise to answer before listening. (Proverbs 18:13)*

to Wise: _____

LIE: *The Lord has made everything for our purpose. (Proverbs 16:4)*

to Wise: _____

LIE: *Being kind to the poor doesn't really matter to God. (Proverbs 19:17)*

to Wise: _____

Proverbs 18

Proverbs 18:4 A person's words can be life-giving water; words of true wisdom are as refreshing as a bubbling brook.

Proverbs 18:7 The mouths of fools are their ruin; their lips get them into trouble.

Proverbs 18:20 Words satisfy the soul as food satisfies the stomach; the right words on a person's lips bring satisfaction.

Proverbs 18:21 Those who love to talk will experience the consequences, for the tongue can kill or nourish life.

I love speaking at mother/daughter events across the country, I especially love getting to meet all the wonderful girls and their mothers. I remember one large event where I was the speaker and after I had finished giving the message, many moms came up to meet me. They had such kind things to say about how God spoke to their hearts through the message I had given and it served as such an encouragement . . . until I met one woman at the end of the line! She had nothing kind to say and began listing her complaints one by one about the entire event. I just stood there for what seemed like forever and tried to be as patient as possible as she went on and on about the sanctuary being too cold, the T-shirts in the bookstore being sold-out of small sizes, and even the sandwich at lunch not having enough lettuce on it! Seriously, I'm not kidding!

Proverbs 18:4 says:

words of true wisdom

I didn't even have control over the temperature in the sanctuary, the T-shirt sizes, or how much lettuce was on the sandwich!

Finally I couldn't take it any longer and I gently interrupted her and said, "I'm just curious, but was there anything positive that God may have shown you that you can take away from this event?" She just stammered and couldn't seem to think of anything! She ended with, "Well, I just thought you should know what was wrong, so you can work to make it better." Um, OK. While I think it's helpful to know when something needs improvement, at the same time, I wondered why this lady couldn't have shared a couple of positive things about the event along with her complaints? Or shared her complaints in a more pleasant tone? Yikes.

What's really crazy is that months after the event ended, I could still remember this one lady's complaints, but I could no longer remember all the wonderful, encouraging comments the other women had made! What's up with that?! I bet you're the same way—it's hard to forget when someone makes a mean, nasty comment even if it's stuck in the middle of a pack of nice ones. The verses above remind us that our words can be "life-giving water" that can "satisfy the soul" and "nourish life." I hope my words spoken to others show up on the list of encouraging comments that bring a smile to their faces. And trust me, when I get a nice card or e-mail from someone who has nice things to say, I save it for a rainy day! You never know when a meanie will come along!

are as refreshing as a bubbling brook

JUST BETWEEN US

1. When was the last time you paid someone a compliment? What was it? How do you think it made them feel at the time?

2. When was the last time someone paid you a compliment? What was it? How did it make you feel at the time?

3. Can you think of a time when someone said something to you that was hurtful? How did it make you feel at the time?

4. What do you think Proverbs 18:21 means when it says, "the tongue can kill or nourish life"? Write it down in your own words.

5. Take a minute to think about the words you speak to others. Do you think they more often kill or nourish life?

PSSST, GOD!

Take a minute and thank God for the advice He gives in His Word. Also thank Him for sending others to give you good advice. Ask Him to help you put aside your pride the next time you are given good advice and follow it.

IN THIS CORNER
WISE WORDS vs LOOSE LIPS

Loose lips sink ships! You may not have ever heard that phrase, but I bet your mom has. The phrase was first said by someone in the United States Office of War Information during World War II to encourage the troops not to talk openly (or have loose lips) about their war plans so enemy spies wouldn't find out and sink the U.S. ships.

The basic meaning is that sometimes opening your mouth, or saying the wrong things can be hurtful to other people. How do you handle your words?

Rate yourself on a scale of 1 to 10 based on how you typically act. The closer to 1 you circle, the closer you typically behave to the sentence on the left and vice versa.

TEAM VIRTUE — STAR PLAYER: WISE WORDS		TEAM VICE — STAR PLAYER: LOOSE LIPS
When asked to do chores, I say "ok" in a sweet tone.	1 2 3 4 5 6 7 8 9 10	When asked to do chores, I usually respond with a whiny "whyyyy?"
I seek out times when I can compliment or encourage my friends.	1 2 3 4 5 6 7 8 9 10	I rarely compliment my friends, and sometimes tease them about things instead.
If someone hurts me and apologizes, I forgive them.	1 2 3 4 5 6 7 8 9 10	When hurt by someone, I hold grudges, even after an apology, and tell them to leave me alone.
If I ask my mom if I can do something and I don't get my way, I accept the decision.	1 2 3 4 5 6 7 8 9 10	If I don't get my way, I ask "Why not?" and say "You *never* let me do/get (fill in the blank)."
When my friends around me say mean things about another girl, I say something nice.	1 2 3 4 5 6 7 8 9 10	When my friends say something mean about another girl, I say "Yeah, I know" and participate in the conversation.

between God & me ✳ proverbs 16–20   (Poster image taken from the Maryland paper, *The News* in 1942)

Often I tell my mom and dad I love them for no reason at all.	1 2 3 4 5 6 7 8 9 10	I never say I love you to my mom and dad first.
When my brothers annoy me, I either don't say anything or ask them nicely to stop.	1 2 3 4 5 6 7 8 9 10	When my brothers annoy me, I immediately yell at them to "Shut up" and tell them why they're so stupid.
When mom is having a hard day, I try to encourage her.	1 2 3 4 5 6 7 8 9 10	When mom is having a bad day, I tend to get frustrated with her or just stay away.
When a girl I don't care for is rude to me, I brush it off saying "I'm sorry you feel that way."	1 2 3 4 5 6 7 8 9 10	When a girl I don't care for is rude to me, I respond by telling her in an angry tone.
When a friend scores badly on a test, I encourage her by saying maybe she'll do better next time.	1 2 3 4 5 6 7 8 9 10	When a friend scores badly on a test, I say "Whoa! That stinks for you!"

Now, total up the numbers you circled to see what corner you're in! How did you do?

KNOCKOUT!

If you scored between 10 and 39, you do a good job of using your words wisely! You see the value of encouragement and try to use your tongue in a positive way. Even though you scored well, take caution! Our tongues are never tamed! (James 3:7–8) Just like some wild animals appear tame, or calm, at any point they can become wild again.

DANCING AROUND THE RING

If you scored between 40 and 70, you probably fall in line with most people (at least those being really honest!) It's not always easy to react or respond with kindness or with calm words. Most of us need to improve in this area, so don't be discouraged. Be on the lookout for someone to encourage this week. And, catch yourself when you are tempted to respond negatively. Keep up this pattern, and soon it will develop into a healthy habit of positive speaking!.

DOWN FOR THE COUNT!

If you scored between 71 and 100, you need to practice holding that tongue of yours! Breathe in, breathe out. If you are a child of God, we must use our tongues to honor Him. Take notice of certain situations where it's harder to react/respond well. Ask Mom and Dad to let you know when you should "try again!" One tip: count to "3 Mississippi" when you're tempted to lash out. And remember, if you can't say something nice, don't say it at all!

Proverbs 19

Proverbs 19:2 It is not good to have zeal without knowledge, nor to be hasty and miss the way.

Proverbs 19:3 A man's own folly ruins his life, yet his heart rages against the LORD.

u will never believe what she did now!!!!!

Raise your hand if you've ever done something really stupid as a result of not taking some time to think it through?

I'm guessing that most of us have our hands up right now, and if you don't, it's just a matter of time.

I remember a guy in my 4th grade homeroom class who did something really, really stupid because he didn't take a minute to think about what he was doing. We were having the end of the year class party and our homeroom mom brought snacks and drinks for the class. The drinks were ice cold Cokes—the kind in the glass bottles! Clay picked up a bottle, took a few sips, and then said, "Hey watch this." He then proceeded to put his index finger into the bottle opening to see if it would fit. It fit all right—so tightly that he couldn't get his finger out! He tugged and tugged, but it didn't help. His finger was a perfect fit in the bottle!

Clay was too embarrassed to tell our teacher, so he walked around with a Coke bottle dangling off his finger for the next hour or so. After awhile his finger began to turn different colors, and he figured he better do something about it. He finally told the teacher and she sent him to the nurse's office. I don't know what kind of magic the nurse did to free his finger from the Coke bottle, but he came back to class about a half hour later with the color back in his finger and a little extra color in his cheeks. How embarrassing!

Proverbs 19 reminds us of the importance of thinking things through, rather than making decisions on the spur of the moment. As you get older, you are going to face many important choices and you will either respond with wisdom (good judgment) or folly. Folly is basically, foolish behavior. Proverbs 19:3 reminds us, "A man's own folly ruins his life, yet his heart rages against the LORD." Some people will actually make poor choices and then turn around and blame God for the results!

God wants to be a part of your everyday life. He wants to walk by your side and help guide you to make wise choices. Like, for example, not putting your finger into a Coke bottle to see if it fits. Cokes were made for drinking, not wearing, right?!

Proverbs 19:8 offers this advice: "Grow a wise heart—you'll do yourself a favor; keep a clear head —you'll find a good life." (The Message)

JUST BETWEEN US

1. Can you think of something foolish you've done, as a result of not taking time to think it through? If so, what was it?

2. Why is it good to stop and think things through before making a choice?

3. What are some steps you can take to "grow a wise heart"?

PSSST, GOD!

Pray and ask God to help you learn to stop and think things through before making decisions rather than rushing into them. When you're facing a decision, ask Him to guide you and give you the wisdom needed.

Quiz

R U a hot-head?

Proverbs 29:22 "An angry man stirs up dissension, and a hot-tempered one commits many sins" (NIV).

Have your parents ever said to you, "Stop overreacting. It's not that big of a deal"? I bet that didn't help your anger in the heat of the moment, did it? Well, like it or not, they are probably right. When it comes to anger, it's easy to overreact to the situation or person. How do you typically react to things when you encounter something that offends you? Let's see!

1. It's time to visit your grandparents, so your family piles into the van for the two-hour trek. About 30 minutes into the trip, your little brother starts to kick the back of your seat. You tell him to stop, but he just kicks harder and harder. You . . .

A) yell "STOP IT" and then stop yourself and ask nicely for him to please stop.

B) scream at the top of your lungs "MIC-HAEL, STOP IT or you'll be sorry!"

C) ask him nicely to stop and when he doesn't, you ask for your mom's help.

2. In English class, you have a test. You didn't really study very much for it and don't feel great about how you did. When you get home, Mom asks how it went. You . . .

A) tell her it went OK, but that there were questions on it that didn't seem fair.

B) tell her that it was really hard, but that you should have spent more time studying.

C) cross your arms and huff while telling how unfair your teacher is and how no one in your class likes her.

3. Your sister "borrows" your headphones and uses them when she goes to the pool with a friend. When she returns them, they reek of her sweat. Grossed out, you . . .

A) march directly to her room and throw the headphones on the bed saying, "YOU messed them up, now YOU have to buy me new ones."

B) ask your sister to please not take your headphones without asking.

C) let her know how frustrated you are and ask her to use her own head-phones next time.

4. You're a star softball player and your team has made it to the semifinals in a weekend tournament. It's down to the last inning, and the referee calls a strike that was TOTALLY a ball. His call causes the batter to walk and the other team to score. You . . .

A) shout "What?!", kick the dirt a little, and then pull it together for the next play.

B) yell to your team, "It's OK guys . . . let's get the next one."

C) throw your glove to the ground, put your hands in the air, and scream "Need some glasses, ref? I can't BELIEVE this! It's so unfair!"

5. Mom says you can't spend the night with Madelyn because you have to be up early for dance class the next day. You . . .

A) are disappointed, but you hold your tongue and try to have a good attitude.

B) roll your eyes, stomp to your room, and slam the door behind you.

C) sigh and say "fine" in a frustrated tone. Later you apologize to her.

6. Everyone is talking in class, but the teacher calls you out. You are the only person to get punished and have to write sentences on the white board. You . . .

A) snap "But Mrs. Cole, everyone was talking. How come I'm the only one who got punished?" Shortly after, you regret saying that and apologize.

B) realize that you were in the wrong, even if no one else got punished and shyly make your way to the board.

C) bark, "What?! This is so unfair!" and stomp to the board in a huff. You look back at your classmates and roll your eyes when your teacher isn't looking.

7. You and your friend, Lindsay, agreed to visit the coolest amusement park together over the summer. You both promised to go with each other. Lindsay ended up getting a free ticket to go with her church youth group and you found out that she was going with them and wasn't planning to tell you. Next time you see her you . . .

A) ask why she didn't tell you. You calmly tell her that it hurt your feelings when you found out about it and ask her if she is still planning to go with you.

B) frown at her and say, "Thanks a lot, Lindsay. Some friend you are!" sarcastically.

C) burst out with, "Lind-say, why are you going without me? You totally ruined everything. I can't believe you!"

8. Jeremy sent a mass e-mail to your entire group of friends retelling an embarrassing story that happened to you earlier that day at school. You reply . . .

A) to the entire group in all CAPS with an equally embarrassing story, and also adding in a few extra things that you know Jeremy wouldn't want other people to know.

B) to the entire group admitting the story, but pointing out that Jeremy was really rude to send it out.

C) to Jeremy and tell him you were hurt by the e-mail. Then, reply again to the group laughing it off and inviting others to share their own embarrassing stories-about themselves!

Total your score by
using points in this legend:

1: a-2
    b-3
    c-1

2: a-1
    b-2
    c-3

3: a-3
    b-1
    c-2

4: a-2
    b-1
    c-3

5: a-1
    b-3
    c-2

6: a-2
    b-1
    c-3

7: a-1
    b-2
    c-3

8: a-3
    b-2
    c-1

How did U score?

Calm, Cool, and Collected!

If you scored between 8 and 11, congratulations! You handle "heated" situations with a lot of "cool"! You realize that even though you may be frustrated on the inside, reacting with a calm tone is always the best choice. You take measures to calm yourself down like counting or waiting to speak. Keep up the good wisdom Miss Calm, Cool, and Collected!

Frustrated but Focused!

If you scored between 12 and 16, you tend to overreact initially in situations, but usually catch yourself before you let it go too far. Initially. You still need some practice working on those initial reactions, which is hard to do. Remember: "a gentle answer quiets wrath!" So, make sure you've dealt with your own anger over a situation before speaking or doing anything, even if it means dismissing yourself to your room for a minute to cool down.

Sizzlin' Hothead!

If you scored between 17 and 24, you, my dear, are a hothead! You let your anger get the best of you and it shows! You don't hold back your anger but let it out, no matter who it hurts in the process. Instead of practicing self-control, you usually end up looking foolish by overreacting. Practice counting to three when you're overly angry or remove yourself entirely from a situation if your temper gets too hot! This takes some major self-control, but the good news is that self-control just happens to be one of the fruits of the Spirit! (Galatians 5:22–23). Pray and ask God to help develop self-control in your life.

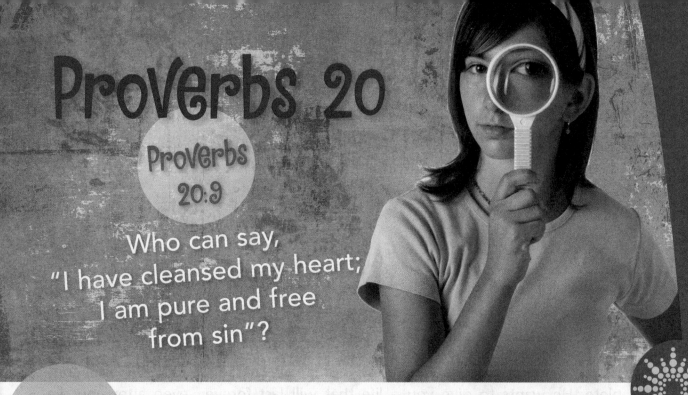

Proverbs 20

Proverbs 20:9

Who can say,
"I have cleansed my heart;
I am pure and free
from sin"?

Have you ever noticed that no one really uses the word *sin* when describing wrong actions? If you look up *sin* in the dictionary, it would say something like "deliberate disobedience to the known will of God." The Bible tells us "for all have sinned and fall short of the glory of God." Basically we are all sinners. If you've done only one wrong thing in your entire life, you're still a sinner. The problem is, God is pure and holy and can't be in the presence of sin. Since God wants to have a relationship with us, He provided a way to remove the sin from our hearts (cleanse us) and make us "pure and free from sin."

When Jesus died on the cross, He died for our sins—past, present, and future. This offer is often called the "great exchange." Basically God exchanges our sins with Christ's righteousness (holiness) and wipes the slate of our hearts clean. That doesn't mean we won't ever sin again. We will continue to have sin in our hearts until we meet Jesus. However, it does mean that when God looks at us, He sees the righteousness of Christ in our hearts. Pretty awesome deal, huh?

When I was in college, I attended an event where someone shared about God's gift and forgiveness. My sin list was pretty long by then and I felt guilty about many of the things I had done. I was relieved to find out about God's gift of forgiveness and bowed my head in prayer that night and told God to count me in.

What about you? If you are not quite sure if you are a Christian, I want you to read what it means to be a Christian on the next few pages. Remember: this is the most important decision you will ever make in your life. No one can make this decision for you. You have to make it on your own. Read very carefully and try to understand what each verse means. Don't worry—we'll take it real slow and go step by step.

We learn about God's love in the Bible

> "For God so loved the world that he gave his one and only Son, that whoever believes in him shall not perish but have eternal life." –John 3:16 (niv)

God loves you. He wants to bless your life and make it happy, full, and complete. He wants to give you a life that will last forever, even after you die. *Perish* means to die and to be apart from God—forever. God wants you to have "eternal life" in heaven where you are with Him forever.

If you understand what John 3:16 means, put a check here: _____

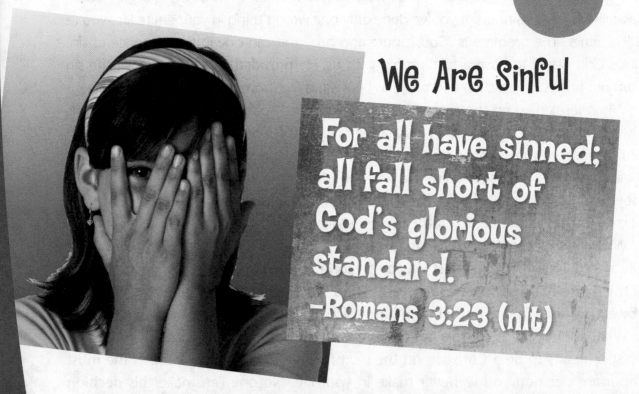

We Are Sinful

> For all have sinned; all fall short of God's glorious standard. –Romans 3:23 (nlt)

You may have heard someone say, "I'm only human—nobody's perfect." This Bible verse says the same thing: We are all sinners. No one is perfect. When we sin, we do things that are wrong—things that God would not agree with. The verse says we fall short of "God's glorious standard." Imagine that

God gives you a test (I know—yuck!). Imagine that you have to make a 100 to meet God's "standard." It makes sense that you have to make a 100 because it's a perfect score and God is perfect. Now let's say that everyone starts with a 100, but anytime you sin (do something wrong), you get a point taken off. Since God is perfect and we are not, it is impossible for anyone to make a 100 on this test! I know it sounds like a strict rule, but think about it. If He is holy and perfect, He can't be around people who are not holy and perfect. If He is, He won't be holy and perfect anymore. But before you start to worry that you don't meet His standard (you won't make a 100), just wait—there's good news ahead.

If you understand what Romans 3:23 means, put a check here: _____

Sin Has a Penalty (punishment)

"For the wages (cost) of sin is death."
–Romans 6:23 (niv)

Just as criminals must pay the penalty for their crimes, sinners must pay the penalty for their sins. Imagine this: What if every time we do something wrong, we get a ticket (kind of like if your mom is speeding in her car and gets a ticket and has to pay money for her punishment). Let's also say that our punishment is not that we have to pay money for our sins, but instead, we have to die. When we die, we will be separated from God for all eternity unless there is a way to pay for our sins (which there is, so don't worry—I'll get to that part!).

If you understand what Romans 6:23 means, put a check here: _____

But God showed his great love for us by sending Christ to die for us while we were still sinners. –Romans 5:8 (nlt)

Christ Has Paid the Price for our Sins!

The Bible teaches that Jesus Christ, the sinless (perfect) Son of God, has paid the price for all your sins. You may think you have to lead a good life and do good deeds before God will love you. It's good to do good deeds, but it won't pay the price for your sins and get you into heaven. But the Bible says that Christ loved you enough to die for you, even when you were acting unlovable. Pretty amazing, huh?!

If you understand what Romans 5:8 means, put a check here: _____

Salvation (life in Heaven) is a Free Gift

God saved you by his special favor when you believed. And you can't take credit for this; it is a gift from God. Salvation is not a reward for the good things we have done, so none of us can boast about it. –Ephesians 2:8-9 (nlt)

The word *grace* means "a gift we don't deserve." It means Christ is offering to pay for something you could never pay for yourself: forgiveness of sins and eternal life, God's gift to you is free. You do not have to work for a gift. That's why it's called a gift. All you have to do is joyfully receive it. Believe with all your heart that Jesus Christ died for you and paid the price for your sins!

If you understand what Ephesians 2:8–9 means, put a check here: _____

Christ Is at Your Heart's Door

"Here I am! I stand at the door and knock. If anyone hears my voice and opens the door, I will come in and eat with him, and he with me." –Revelation 3:20 (niv)

Jesus Christ wants to have a personal relationship with you. He wants to be your very best friend. He wants you to talk to Him just like you would talk to your best friend. Picture, if you will, Jesus Christ standing at the door of your heart and knocking. Invite Him in; He is waiting for you to receive Him into your heart and life.

If you understand what Revelation 3:20 means,

put a check here: _____

You Must Receive Him

But to all who believed him and accepted him, he gave the right to become children of God.–John 1:12 (nlt)

When you receive Christ into your heart you become a child of God, and you can talk to Him in prayer at any time about anything. The Christian life is a personal relationship (just like you have with your parents or best friend) with God through Jesus Christ. And best of all, it is a relationship that will last forever and ever. There is nothing you could ever do to make God stop loving you. Even though we will continue to sin from time to time, God still loves us. He never takes His gift back, so we don't have to worry about losing it. It is ours to keep forever.

If you understand what John 1:12 means,
put a check here: _____

So, what do you think about God's gift of forgiveness? If after reading through the verse above, you feel that God is drawing you to accept this gift, tell Him. You don't have to say a fancy prayer—just talk to Him and tell Him that you believe that Jesus died on the cross for your sins and you want to accept that gift. That's all it takes! What are you waiting for? Stop and say a prayer right now.

Did you say a prayer and accept God's gift of forgiveness? _____

If you answered "yes," congratulations! You are a Christian! If you did not understand some of the verses above and you aren't quite sure you are ready to accept God's gift of forgiveness, please talk to someone who can help you understand what it means to be a Christian. Maybe it's your Pastor, parents, or a relative. Maybe it's your friend's mom. Find someone who knows what it means to be a Christian and tell them you want to know more!

JUST BETWEEN US

1. Has there been a time in your life when you prayed and accepted God's gift of forgiveness? If so, tell me about it.

2. If you have not made that decision, how do you feel after reading the steps to becoming a Christian on the previous pages?

3. If you prayed to receive Christ after reading through the steps, I want you to think of at least one person you can tell about your decision who will celebrate the news with you. Who would that be?

4. The steps to becoming a Christian are often referred to as the "Good News." Why do you think that is?

5. Who are some people you know that need to hear the "Good News"? Will you tell them?

PSSST, GOD!

If you followed the steps above and prayed to receive God's gift of forgiveness through His Son, Jesus Christ, take a minute and thank God for your new life in Christ. If you are already a Christian, take a minute and thank God for sending His Son to die on the cross for your sins. Now, pray for some of your friends who need to hear the "Good News" and receive Christ as their Savior.

(Above was adapted from "Your Christian Life" 1965, 1968, as "Aids to Christian Living," 1986 as "Practical Steps in Christian Living," 1995 as "Beginning Your Christian Life," 1997 as "Your Christian Life," Billy Graham Evangelistic Association)

My child, listen and be wise. Keep your heart on the right course.

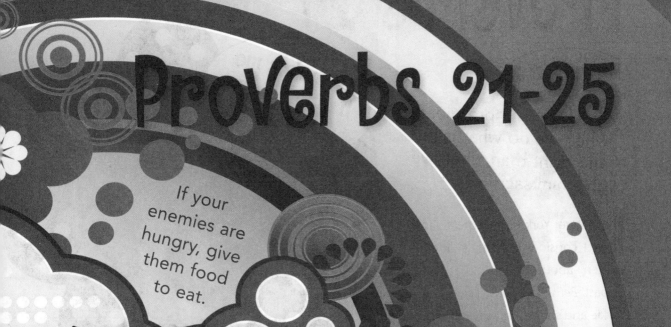

Proverbs 21-25

If your enemies are hungry, give them food to eat.

Choose a good reputation over great riches.

The LORD is more pleased when we do what is just and right than when we give him sacrifices.

Proverbs 21

Proverbs 21:3

The LORD is more pleased when we do what is just and right than when we give him sacrifices.

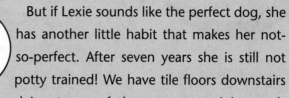

It makes me happy to give you my toy!

I have two Yorkshire Terriers (Yorkies) that I consider my "fur children." I've written about Lexie and Scout before in past *Between* books. Lexie is my older Yorkie and she's about seven years old. She loves to play with sqeaky toys, especially if I'll grab the other end and play a game of tug-of-war with her. Sometimes, when she's done playing and all pooped out, she'll jump up on my chair with her favorite squeaky toy and do the cutest thing. She'll drop it in my lap and then lie down beside me to sleep. The first time she put the toy in my lap, I thought she wanted to play some more. I waved it in front of her to see if she wanted to play tug-of-war, but she just ignored me and closed her eyes! After she did it a few more times, I finally figured out that she was leaving the toy in my lap as a gift, trusting me with it while she sleeps. It's the only thing of value she has to offer her master and it's her way of saying, *"Hey thanks for taking care of me, feeding me, and loving me."*

. . . but I want to do things MY way!

But if Lexie sounds like the perfect dog, she has another little habit that makes her not-so-perfect. After seven years she is still not potty trained! We have tile floors downstairs and I put one of those puppy training pads down each morning just in case the dogs can't hold it until we go outside for a walk. My other dog, Scout, (who is younger) faithfully goes on the puppy pad. Lexie, however, goes right beside the potty pad on the tile floor . . . almost every day. Ugh. It is so frustrating! I've tried everything to get her potty trained, but nothing seems to work. I patiently take her over to the puppy pad each morning to show her where to go, put her in the pen when she disobeys, and give her treats when she hits the mark . . . which is a rare occurrence. Yet day after day, I walk into the room and see another piddle puddle!

I kind of feel the same way about Lexie that God feels about us when we disobey. Proverbs 21:3 reminds us, "The LORD is more pleased when we do what is just and right than when we give him sacrifices." As sweet as it is when Lexie drops her toy in my lap as a present, I would much rather she just obey me and go potty on the puppy pad! I know she doesn't understand people talk, but I just want to scream, *"Keep your present and obey—that's the best present you could give me!"* Hmmm . . . I wonder if God feels the same way about our sacrifices?

YIKES!
God's word says that He would rather me do the right thing than give up my toys!

JUST BETWEEN US

1. What are some sacrifices you have given to the Lord? (Examples: Giving your money at church, donating canned foods or clothes to the poor, going on mission trips, etc.)

2. How do you feel after you've done something that is sacrificial to the Lord?

3. While God is certainly pleased with your sacrifices, what does He value even more?

4. No one is perfect, and God knows that. He knows that we won't always do what is "right and just." However, it's a good idea to apologize to Him when we make mistakes and show sorrow for our mistakes. Are you in the habit of doing that?

PSSST, GOD!

Pray and ask God to show you areas of your life where you frequently disobey Him or His standards in the Bible. Now, ask Him to give you the wisdom to make good choices and the strength to follow through.

Say WHAT?

Better to live on a corner of the roof than share a house with a quarrelsome wife. (Proverbs 21:9 NIV)

Drip, drip, drip

At first glance, this verse may sound like it's a permission slip to send Mom to the roof when she quarrels with you about cleaning your room for the bazillionith time! Sorry, but it's actually a verse about wives, so you're out of luck! What it's basically saying is that it would be better for a husband to live all cramped up in a tiny corner of the roof than with a nagging, quarrelsome wife. Ouch!

Proverbs 27:15 also talks about "nagging wives" and says, *"A quarrelsome wife is like a constant dripping on a rainy day"* (NIV). You might wonder why I'm including this verse on "wives" when you're not yet old enough for it to apply. The truth is, it's never too early to learn truths in the Bible. Quarrelsome little girls often grow up to become quarrelsome wives. And I don't know about you, but I don't want to send my husband running for the corner of the roof! This verse is a great training verse for you wives-in-waiting so keep these hidden in your heart! :)

Have you ever stopped to think about what our lives would be like if we didn't have teeth? Ever have a toothache where you couldn't chew on one side of your mouth? Ouch! If you've had that happen, you know how annoying it can be to have to learn to chew your food on the other side of your mouth. But what if you had no teeth like some old people? They have to get dentures just to help them chew their food and spend more time and effort getting the job done.

Or have you ever had a sprained ankle? You don't realize how much it can slow you down until you have to hobble around on crutches for a few weeks. The Bible verse on the rights reminds us that counting on people who are not dependable is as annoying as chewing your food with a bad tooth or trying to walk with an injured foot. It's a PAIN to count on people who let you down over and over again.

Like a bad tooth or a lame foot is reliance on the unfaithful in times of trouble. (Proverbs 25:19 NIV)

Like one who takes away a garment on a cold day, or like vinegar poured on soda, is one who sings songs to a heavy heart. (Proverbs 25:20)

Yikes!

Do you have an annoying sibling (or maybe classmate) who, when you're feeling sad or grumpy, they seem to take joy in seeing you miserable? Maybe you're upset about something and this person continually talks about it just to annoy you. They know it's the last thing you want to talk about. Or, maybe you get punished and lose a privilege (like watching TV) and your brother or sister rubs it in that THEY still get to enjoy watching TV. Ugh.

The verse above says that when someone takes away a garment on a cold day (brrrrr!) or pours vinegar on soda (ick!), it's the same as when someone sings songs to a heavy heart. Basically, it's the opposite of what the person needs at the time. When someone is troubled, or deeply sad/upset, we should not add more pain to their situation by annoying them. Instead, we should be sympathetic to their pain and grieve with them. Romans 12:15 says, "Rejoice with those who rejoice; mourn with those who mourn" (NIV). So, remember to be respectful when people are hurting, and let them have some time to process their feelings. Sometimes, a simple, "Hey, I'm sorry you're sad," is all they really need to get past it.

Proverbs 22

Proverbs 22:1
Choose a good reputation over great riches, for being held in high esteem is better than having silver or gold

When I was in 2nd grade, I remember a contest that my homeroom teacher held at the end of the year party. She brought a giant, monster-size jar of gumballs and placed it on her desk. She then handed us each a slip of paper and told us to "estimate" how many gumballs were in the jar and write it down on the slip of paper. The person whose number came the closest to the actual number of gumballs would get to take home the whole jar as a prize! She gave us a few minutes to study the jar and no one made a sound. I mean, we're talking about a summer-long supply of gumballs—who doesn't want to win that, right?!

Finally I came up with a number and wrote it down on my slip of paper. The homeroom mother gathered them up and then announced the number of gumballs. Unfortunately I didn't win, but my best friend did! Of course, that meant that I was sure to get my hands on some of those gumballs over the summer, so I was happy for her. We would just have to figure out a good hiding place for the jar, so her pesky little brother wouldn't find it!

My friend won the jar of gumballs because her estimated number came closest to the actual number of gumballs in the jar. You've probably learned to estimate numbers in math class, but did you know that it's also possible to "estimate" people? For example, if I call out the names of a few of the most popular Disney Channel celebrities and ask you to think of two or three words to describe each person's character, you could probably think of the words pretty quickly. And the words you think of would help estimate that character's "reputation."

I'm not sure if the word "reputation" has appeared on your list of spelling words yet, but it's a word that every young person needs to know about. The dictionary defines "reputation" as the "accepted estimation of someone." Basically everyone has a reputation. For example, I had a friend in third grade who loved to play board games whenever I went over to her house. However, there was one little problem: Whenever she saw that she might lose the game, she would quit and say she wanted to do something else. It drove me crazy! After awhile, I got tired of it and quit going over to her house. When my mom asked me why I didn't want to go, I told her that she didn't play fair and it wasn't fun anymore. She found new friends to invite over, but it was only a matter of time before they too began to complain about her being a sore loser. Basically she ended up getting a reputation for not playing fair, and as a result, she had a hard time making and keeping friends. After awhile no one wanted to go to her house because it was such a frustrating experience. How sad that in the end, she cared more about losing a silly board game than losing her friends!

Reputation: the accepted estimation of someone

JUST BETWEEN US

1. Let me ask you a hard question: What is your reputation? If we asked your friends and classmates to think of two or three words to describe you, what might they say?

2. What kind of words would you hope your friends and classmates might use to describe you?

3. Overall, would you say that your reputation is good or bad?

4. We all have areas that we need to work on in our lives. What might be something that you need to work on to become a better friend/person?

PSSST, GOD!

Ask God to give you a desire to have a good name and a good reputation. If you're worried that the estimation others may have of you is not a positive one, ask Him to give you the strength to change your ways. Seek to be pleasing in His eyes and you can't go wrong!

LIES to WISE

Look up the verses below and rewrite them to change the LIES back into Wise Bible verses!

LIE: *A man's ways seem right to him, and God agrees. (Proverbs 21:2)*

to Wise: _____

LIE: *We should ignore wisdom and trust in ourselves. (Proverbs 22:17-19)*

to Wise: _____

LIE: *When your enemy or fails, rejoice because he/she had it coming! (Proverbs 24:17)*

to Wise: _____

LIE: *Being boastful will bring honor and life. (Proverbs 22:4)*

to Wise: _____

LIE: *Finding wisdom leads to hopelessness and depression. (Proverbs 24:14)*

to Wise: _____

LIE: *Training a child in the way of God's truth isn't that important. (Proverbs 22:6)*

to Wise: _____

LIE: *A wise person is powerless and wimpy. (Proverbs 24:5)*

to Wise: _____

LIE: *Life, prosperity (happiness) and honor are found when you pursue hatred and sin. (Proverbs 21:21)*

to Wise: _____

Proverbs 23

Proverbs 23:15 My child, how I will rejoice if you become wise.

Proverbs 23:16 Yes, my heart will thrill when you speak what is right and just.

Proverbs 23:17 Don't envy sinners, but always continue to fear the LORD.

Proverbs 23:18 For surely you have a future ahead of you; your hope will not be disappointed.

Proverbs 23:19 My child, listen and be wise. Keep your heart on the right course.

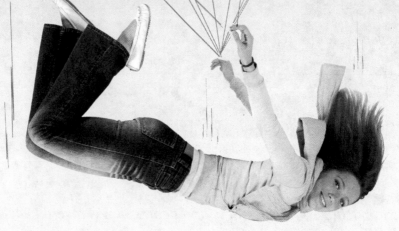

There is a story told about four people flying in a small, four-passenger plane: a pilot, a minister, and two teenagers, one of whom had just won an award for being the "Smartest Teenager in the World."

As they were flying along, the pilot turned to the three passengers and said, "I've got some bad news, and I've got some worse news. The bad news is, we're out of gas. The plane's going down and we're gonna crash. The worse news is, I only have three parachutes on board."

This meant, of course, that someone would have to go down with the plane. The pilot continued. "I have a wife and three children at home. I have many responsibilities. I'm sorry, but I'm going to have to take one of the parachutes." With that, he grabbed one of the chutes and jumped out of the plane.

The Smartest Teenager in the World was next to speak. "I'm the Smartest Teenager in the World," he said. "I might be the one who comes up with a cure for cancer or AIDS or solves the world's economic problems. Everyone is counting on me!" The Smartest Teenager in the World grabbed the second parachute and jumped.

The minister then spoke up and said, "Son, you take the last parachute. I've made my peace with God, and I'm willing to go down with the plane. Now take the last parachute and go."

"Relax, reverend," said the other teenager. "The Smartest Teenager in the World just jumped out of the plane with my backpack."

Of course the story is not true but was meant to make a point. As you grow up, you'll meet many smart people. Maybe you're one of them! However, being smart doesn't always make you wise. Proverbs 23:15 reminds us that God will "rejoice if you become wise." Did you catch that? It didn't say, "I will rejoice if you made straight A's" or "I will rejoice if you make the Honor Roll."

Now, take a look at verse 16. Does it say, "My heart will thrill when you make a 100 on the spelling test?" Or did it say, "My heart will thrill when your project wins a ribbon in the Science Fair?" No! It says, "My heart will thrill when you speak what is right and just."

Being smart may earn you good grades, academic awards, college scholarships, and possibly a good job someday. But, being smart doesn't guarantee you a happy future. If you want a future and a hope, listen and be wise. Keep your heart on the right course. You don't want to be the one grabbing the backpack . . . go for the parachute!

JUST BETWEEN US

1. Can you think of someone you know (don't mention names), who is smart and makes good grades, but doesn't have much common sense or wisdom?

2. What do you think is more important in our world today: Being smart or being wise? Why?

3. Have you ever been to an awards ceremony where someone was rewarded for having wisdom and making good choices?

4. If God hands out awards in heaven, what do you think would be more important to Him: intelligence or wisdom?

PSSST, GOD!

Pray and ask God to help you gain wisdom. Ask Him to help you learn to listen for His voice and keep your heart on the right course.

IN THIS CORNER

GENEROSITY vs GREED

TEAM VIRTUE
STAR PLAYER:
GENEROSITY
VS
TEAM VICE
STAR PLAYER:
GREED

A few years ago there was a TV game show called "Greed." The basic idea of the show was that contestants participated on teams to answer trivia questions and win money. The captain of the team would decide the final answer for the team and whether or not they would risk losing all the money they had earned to try for the next level and a chance to earn more money. It was very tempting because who doesn't want to win more money. Many times their greed (or a strong craving for money or things) would win out over common sense and they would end up losing everything!

We can be very greedy with resources, or things, that God has given us. Greed is especially hard to resist in a world where everything is at our fingertips! Think about it. You can get just about anything with a click of the mouse (even a piece of gum chewed by a celebrity . . . eee-www!). The opposite of greed is generosity. There are a lot of ways we can be generous: through donating our money, things, or even our time! How do you measure up? Do you tend to be greedy or generous?

Rate yourself on a scale of 1 to 10 based on how you typically act. The closer to 1 you circle, the closer you typically behave to the sentence on the left and vice versa.

 (Poster image taken from the Maryland paper, *The News* in 1942)

Helps others by donating items to local charities	1 2 3 4 5 6 7 8 9 10	Keeps everything you have
Often shares with friends without being asked	1 2 3 4 5 6 7 8 9 10	Only shares with friends when you have to
Sometimes uses allowance money to buy things for others	1 2 3 4 5 6 7 8 9 10	Likes to see allowance pile up so you can spend it on yourself
Automatically takes the smaller half of the cookie when sharing with a friend	1 2 3 4 5 6 7 8 9 10	Automatically snatches the larger half of the cookie when sharing with a friend
Participates in service projects through church, school or with family	1 2 3 4 5 6 7 8 9 10	Never participates in service projects and uses all spare time on self
Thinks of money as a gift from God	1 2 3 4 5 6 7 8 9 10	Thinks of money as something you earned
Lets a friend pick first when choosing between two things	1 2 3 4 5 6 7 8 9 10	Always picks first so you can get your way
Splits your last piece of gum with your friend	1 2 3 4 5 6 7 8 9 10	Quickly sneaks the last piece of gum in your mouth so you don't have to share
Gives a portion of money to church	1 2 3 4 5 6 7 8 9 10	Never gives money to church . . . you earned it
Constantly thinks of ways to bless others (maybe through small gifts like crafts, artwork, or even kind words)	1 2 3 4 5 6 7 8 9 10	Never thinks about how to bless others

Here's a twist: go back through the inventory and replace the word "friend" with "brother" or "sister" or even "oh-so annoying person in your grade" to see if you still score in the same category! It's a lot harder to be generous to our siblings or those we don't always get along with, isn't it!?!?

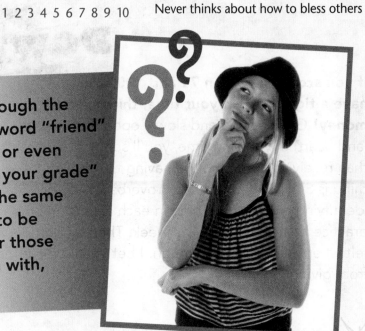

Now, total up the numbers you circled to see what corner you're in! How did you do?

**If you scored between 10 and 39,
you understand that God has given you many things in your life to be shared.**
It's important to you to honor God with those resources and recognize that they really all belong to Him anyway. When given choices to be generous or greedy, you most often pick generous! Way to go!

**If you scored between 40 and 70,
you could use a little nudge to develop a more generous heart.**
You are giving to others in some areas, but still need to improve in other areas. Identify the one area that is hardest for you when it comes to being generous and come up with three things you can do this month to work on it!

If you scored between 71 and 100, you have a tight grip on your time, things, and money! Girl, ease up and slowly open that hand (and heart) of yours! In time, you'll see that giving is truly more exciting than receiving. Even though having things is not always bad, too much of a good thing is STILL too much (see Proverbs 24:16, 27). Start honoring God today by identifying at least one thing in each area (time, money and things) where you can practice being generous this week. Then, underneath each one, record how you felt when you followed through. I bet you'll be surprised at the blessing you receive from giving!

Proverbs 24

Proverbs 24:19 Do not fret because of evildoers; don't envy the wicked.

Proverbs 24:20 For the evil have no future; their light will be snuffed out.

Proverbs 24:29 And don't say, "Now I can pay them back for all their meanness to me! I'll get even!"

You've probably heard of the Disney Channel sensation, Demi Lovato. But did you know that the Camp Rock star was severely bullied in the seventh grade? In fact, the bullying became so unbearable that her mother eventually removed her from the school and home-schooled her, so she could focus on school and her budding career.

"I never really understood why [I was being bullied] until looking back," says Lovato, who suspects her classmates were jealous she was a child star. *"I had a different lifestyle than everyone else."* I have no doubts that 7th-grade girls at Demi's school were probably green with envy over the fact that she was an actress. What is it that makes some girls want to bring other girls down when they are successful? Is it so they can feel better about themselves?

Of course, I'm one to talk. When I was in 7th grade, I was super jealous when my best friend made the cut of fifteen girls during cheerleader tryouts and I didn't. When the fifteen girls tried out in front of the student body the following week for the final six spots, I couldn't even bring myself to vote for her! Of course, I feel horrible about it now and realize that instead of being jealous, I should have celebrated with her and rallied others to vote for her.

Oh, and get this: We both made it the following year and she was super happy for me, which of course made me feel even worse!

When others hurt you, it's hard to take the high road and do nothing to pay them back. God wants us to lay our troubles at His feet and trust Him to take care of matters for us. Sometimes it's necessary to involve trusted adults like our mother or a teacher to help find a solution to the problem if it gets really out of hand. Demi Lovato didn't do anything to retaliate against the mean girls she encountered in the 7th grade, but God took care of it. I imagine that every time they see her on TV or hear one of her songs on the radio, they think, *"Hmmm . . . maybe I should have been nicer to that girl!"* Who knows, maybe one of the perks of being her friend is meeting the Jonas Brothers!

1. Have you ever had a situation where someone was jealous of you? What happened? (Remember, don't mention specific names if you are answering these questions in a group.)

2. How did you respond to the situation above? Did you do anything to get the person back?

3. Can you think of a time when you or someone you know chose not to "get the other person back" for something mean and God took care of the matter? If yes, what happened?

4. What do you think it means in Proverbs 24:19 when it says, "Do not fret because of evildoers"?

Stop for a minute and talk to God about the mean girls in your school or church. Ask Him to help you keep a low profile and avoid their acts of meanness. Ask Him to give you the strength to give the matter over to Him to handle rather than retaliate by being mean in return.

MAD LiPS

What do your words say about you?
Finish this story to find out if you're
a sweet talker
or cheap talker!

Being in the _____ grade isn't easy. Especially when
(grade you're in)

_____, who is the meanest girl in _____ grade.
(a girl's name)   *(grade you're in)*

She's a real "MG" (Mean Girl.) It just so happens that you and your

BFF, _____, are both trying out
(name of one of your BFFs)

for the advanced _____ class.
(type of dance)

They only accept _____ students in a semester. You and
(number between 10 and 20)

_____ have both dreamed about making the class for _____
(same name of one of your BFFs)   *(number from 1-12)*

months and already talked about practicing after school every day together.

_____ is a really _____ dancer, but she is NOT
(name of MG)   *(adjective like "awesome" or "great")*

a nice person! She constantly teased you about your_____
                                                         (body part)

saying it's grody and_____. On the day they post the results,
                                (adjective like "gross")

you,_____, and _____ all show up at
(same name of one of your BFFs)   *(name of MG)*

the same time! You see it! There's your name, _____ on the list!
                                             (order like 1st, 2nd, etc)

You quickly scan the list and do not find

either _____'s or
(same name of one of your BFFs)

_____'s name. Neither
(name of MG)

made the class. Disappointed, you

turn to _____ and say,
(BFF name)

"_____

_____."
(something nice you would say to
someone to console them)

Then, you see _____
(name of MG)

out of the corner of your eye.

This is your chance to get her back for all the nasty things she said
about you. You realize it's wrong, but surely she deserves it. You
finally decide to say,

"_____

_____."
(something nice you would say to someone to console them OR a
phrase you might say to someone when you get revenge for something)

What did you say to MG?

If you treated MG the same way that you treated your BFF, then you're a
sweet talker! You hold your tongue when tempted to say something bad,
even when it seems like the perfect time to get revenge! No matter what the
situation, you realize that your words have power and it's always best to be
kind, even if someone's not kind to you!

If you got revenge and rubbed it in MG's face that she didn't make the class,
then you're a cheap talker! You took the opportunity to hurt her with your
words like she did to you with her words. Even though it's tempting, it's not
the wisest or most Christlike response. Practice holding that tongue of yours
until you can use it for good!

Proverbs 25

Proverbs 25:21   If your enemies are hungry, give them food to eat. If they are thirsty, give them water to drink.

Proverbs 25:22   You will heap burning coals on their heads, and the LORD will reward you.

When my daughter was seven years old, she was in a gymnastics class that met several times a week. Some of the girls in the class who mastered the harder skills were chosen to perform on a show team. After watching the show team perform, Paige was determined to be a part of the team. She worked very hard to master the skills and finally she was asked to join the team.

Her first few weeks of practicing with the girls on the show team were pretty rough. She was the "new girl" and oftentimes the other girls would leave her out. One girl in particular was especially mean to Paige. She would tease Paige when she would try a new trick and point and laugh at her when she tumbled down the mat. Sometimes she would cut in front of Paige in line and tell the other girls to do the same thing. Finally my daughter just couldn't take it any longer. She burst into tears one night at bedtime and told me she wanted to quit the show team because of "mean Robin."

I wanted so badly to call Robin's mother or the show team coach, but I decided to pray with Paige first and see if we couldn't solve the problem by looking into God's Word for a solution. I shared with Paige that Matthew 5:44 says, "But I tell you: Love your enemies and pray for those who persecute you" (NIV). If you look the word *persecute* up in the dictionary, you would find a definition that says, "to annoy or trouble persistently." So we decided to pray for Robin. After we were done praying, Paige shockingly said, "Mom, I know! I can make a card for Robin!"

Love your enemies and pray for those who persecute you.

GOd
BLESS
you!

The next day she gathered up all her craft supplies and went to work making Robin a card. She even tucked in some stickers that a friend had just given her as part of her birthday present. The next day we headed off to practice with the card in hand. We got there a little early, so she could give the card to Robin before class started. When Robin walked into the door, I said a silent prayer for my daughter as she walked over to hand it to her.

Slowly Robin opened the card, read the sweet message inside, and then saw the stickers. I could hardly believe what happened next: a smile broke out across her face and she walked over and hugged Paige! After that, she was much nicer to Paige. They didn't become best friends, but there was peace during practice. While I can't promise you that making a card for your "enemy" will bring you the same results, I can promise you this:

If you pray for the people who persecute you and give the matter over to God instead of taking revenge, you will certainly bring a smile to His face. :)

JUST BETWEEN US

1. Can you think of a time when someone was mean to you and you wanted to be mean back? What happened and how did you respond? (Remember, don't share names if you're doing this in a group!)

2. Did you pray about the above situation and ask God to help you through it?

3. Is there someone in your life right now who is mean to you? If so, are you open to praying for that person?

4. My daughter was able to "love her enemy" by making a card for her when she didn't deserve it. Can you think of a way to "love your enemy?" (If you have "an enemy" right now.)

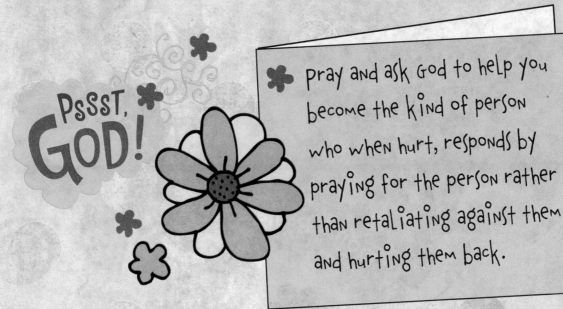

PSSST, GOD!

❋ pray and ask God to help you become the kind of person who when hurt, responds by praying for the person rather than retaliating against them and hurting them back.

Don't praise yourself; let others do it!

Charm is deceptive, and beauty does not last; but a woman who fears the LORD will be greatly praised.

Proverbs 26-31

Proverbs 26

Proverbs 26:18 Just as damaging as a mad man shooting a lethal weapon

Proverbs 26:19 is someone who lies to a friend and then says, "I was only joking."

Proverbs 26:20 Fire goes out for lack of fuel, and quarrels disappear when gossip stops.

Proverbs 26:21 A quarrelsome person starts fights as easily as hot embers light charcoal or fire lights wood.

WARNING: TOO MUCH TIME SPENT WITH THE FOLLOWING TYPES OF FRIENDS CAN BE DANGEROUS TO YOUR HEALTH:

THE JOKER:

This person likes to say things that are often mean and hurtful and then cover it up with "Just kidding!"

THE WHISPERER:

This person always knows the latest scoop and is willing to share it to a listening ear.

THE BOXER:

This person loves a good fight . . . so much so that she looks for ways to start one just for the sake of drama.

As you read these descriptions, some of the girls you know may have come to mind . . . or maybe you saw yourself in one of the descriptions. I'm not saying to cut ties with any friend who shows one little sign of being like one of the descriptions above. We've all probably been guilty of matching one or more of the descriptions above at some point. I just think it's a good idea to keep a distance from girls who show a pattern of behaving like one of these three descriptions.

Let's try this: Match the below symptoms with one of the following types of friends:

J = JOKER
W = WHISPERER
B = BOXER

___ Hey, did you hear about . . . but, don't tell anyone I told you!

___ Nice swimsuit. I had one like that when I was five years old. Just kidding!

___ Her mom told my mom and my mom told me, but no one is supposed to know.

___ I hate her! She's always starting drama!

___ Well, at least I didn't flunk the spelling test! only kidding.

___ Gosh. She makes me so mad. Let's tell everyone to ignore her at lunch.

___ oooh, nice haircut. Don't worry, it'll grow out! JK!

___ I am not inviting her to my party. That'll show her. We should all talk about the party in front of her just to make her mad.

___ So-and-so told me that she told her that she likes him. I kinda hope he finds out. But don't tell anyone I told you.

Hopefully doing this matching game gave you a better idea of how to identify potentially dangerous friendships. Remember, we've all probably been guilty of behaving like a Joker, Whisperer, or Boxer at some point. The main concern is whether or not the behavior has become a pattern. Change is always possible but only if the person who needs to change is aware they have a problem and willing to do something about it. You can't change other people, but you can pray that God will change them!

1. Read Proverbs 26:18–19 on page 126. Circle the type of friend it describes:

JOKER　　WHISPERER　　BOXER

2. Read Proverbs 26:20 on page 126. Circle the type of friend it describes:

JOKER　　WHISPERER　　BOXER

3. Read Proverbs 26:21 on page 126. Circle the type of friend it describes:

JOKER　　WHISPERER　　BOXER

4. Have any of your friends recently made comments like the ones you read in the matching game on page 127? If so, what was the comment that they made? How did you respond to the comment? Now that you think about it, what might be the best way to respond in the future if your friend says something that crosses the line again?

PSSST, GOD!

If while reading the descriptions above, you realized that you may fit the description of the Joker, Whisperer, or Boxer, pray and ask God to help you change. If you have a friend who meets the description, pray for your friend. And remember, if she gets worse, you might want to keep a distance.

Say WHAT?

Like one who seizes a dog by the ears is a passer-by who meddles in a quarrel not his own.
(Proverbs 26:17 NIV)

Are you a dog lover? One of my favorite things to do is to find that sweet spot near a dog's ear and rub it until his little legs shake in utter bliss or he leans so far into my hand that he loses all sense of balance. Now, we know that dogs' ears are for rubbing, but what would happen if you pulled them hard and tried to use them like a leash? I bet you'd find out pretty quickly that sweet little Rover has a mean streak and a pretty wicked bite. Now, think about doing that to a total stranger's dog! Yikes! Can we all agree that it would be just plain S-T-U-P-I-D?

Well, that's what it's like to meddle in a quarrel that doesn't involve you. To meddle means to interfere and put yourself in a situation that doesn't even involve you. Simply put, we need to mind our own business! Sometimes this is very hard to do, especially among a group of girls. Many times, you find out about something that has happened, and you try to either A) fix it, or B) take sides, or C) get other people involved. Do the S-M-A-R-T thing and stay out of battles that aren't yours to fight!

When I first read this verse, I was convinced that it is proof that God wants us to sleep late in the mornings! Okay, maybe not. I am NOT a morning person, so I thought this was an excuse for me to keep hitting the snooze button on my alarm clock!

When you take a closer look at the verse, it's actually talking about people who offer public praise in a show-offy way to get others to notice them. That doesn't mean it's wrong to offer people praises, but we need to make sure that we do it in a way that wouldn't draw attention away from God or draw attention to us.

If a man loudly blesses his neighbor early in the morning, it will be taken as a curse. (Proverbs 27:14 NIV)

BLAH, BLAH, BLAH

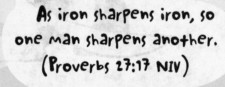

As iron sharpens iron, so one man sharpens another. (Proverbs 27:17 NIV)

Have you ever seen someone sharpen a knife? Maybe you've caught a glance at a cooking show on TV and noticed a chef using that silver wand looking thing against the blade of the knife back and forth, back and forth, getting it as sharp as possible to cut something up. To effectively sharpen iron, you must use iron.

The above verse applies to our spiritual growth, and how God chooses to use other people in the process to help us grow and know Him better. Just as iron is sharpened by iron, the same is true for people. We are "sharpened" spiritually by other people who are as strong or stronger than us spiritually. We grow in our faith and become more mature in Christ when we allow others to help us improve in areas where we need some help. And sometimes we are the one that God uses to do the "sharpening" in someone else's life. Are you open to being "sharpened" by others and "sharpening" others? If so, no one can say you're "dull"! (Ha!)

Proverbs 27

Proverbs 27:2 Don't praise yourself; let others do it!

Proverbs 27:21 Fire tests the purity of silver and gold, but a person is tested by being praised.

DON'T PRAISE YOURSELF!

One afternoon my daughter (who was in high school at the time) and I stepped into a Christian bookstore near our house to take a look around. Actually, I had a new book that had just released and I wanted to sneak in and check to see if the bookstore was carrying it. I told my daughter, "Shhh . . . we're just checking to see if it's on the shelves, but don't say anything about me being an author." It was kind of like we were on a secret mission. Sneak in and check, and then sneak out. We headed to the section where they stocked the youth books and there it was! It's always cool when you're an author and you see your book on the store shelves. I gave my daughter a silent thumb's up signal and she smiled. Even though I had a copy at home, I picked it up and began thumbing through the pages while my daughter was busy looking at some other books on the shelf.

About that time the store manager appeared by my side and noticing the book I was thumbing through, he said, *"You know, that book is written by a local author who lives right here in town."* I could sense my daughter about to crack up laughing right beside me, so I quickly shot her a warning glare. You know the kind I'm talking about . . . where your mom doesn't even have to use words, you just KNOW you better zip your lip! Then the manager continued, *"In fact, Vicki Courtney has written quite a few books that your daughter might enjoy."* No way. Please tell me he did not just say that.

At that point I didn't even have to look over at my daughter. I KNEW she was cracking up. In fact, she was so tickled that she walked around the corner to hide her face and finish off her little laugh-fest.

I acted very interested in what the manager was telling me and thanked him for the advice, but I didn't feel comfortable saying that I was Vicki Courtney. And besides, how do I explain thumbing through my own book?! After he walked away, I rounded the corner to look for my daughter only to find her practically doubled over on the floor trying to hold her laughter in as best as she could. *"Mom, why didn't you tell him you were the author?" "Shhh . . . ,"* I interrupted. *"I don't want to sound like I'm bragging."* At that point I grabbed her hand, squeezed it hard, and told her it was time to head out before she blew our cover. Mission accomplished! Game over!

JUST BETWEEN US

ABOUT BRAGGING . . .

1. Can you think of a time when you or someone you know bragged about something? If so, what was said? (Don't use names if you're sharing this in a group!)

2. Can you think of a time when you were tempted to brag about something, but you stopped yourself just in time and didn't say anything? Describe the situation.

3. Can you think of a time when someone else bragged on you for something? Describe the situation. How did it feel? Did it feel better than if you had done the bragging yourself?

4. Why do you think some people like to brag about themselves?

PSSST, GOD!

Pray and ask God to help you hold your tongue when you're tempted to brag. Besides, a compliment is always sweeter when it comes from someone else!

Look up the verses below and rewrite them to change the *LIES* back into **Wise** Bible verses!

LIE: A fool learns from his/her mistakes. (Proverbs 26:11)

to Wise: _____

LIE: A wise man trusts in himself. (Proverbs 28:26)

to Wise: _____

LIE: Gossiping is usually harmless fun. (Proverbs 26:22)

to Wise: _____

LIE: Having a reverent (or tender, respectful) heart toward the Lord brings sadness and confusion. (Proverbs 27:14)

to Wise: _____

LIE: Virtuous girls love to be dishonest and tell lies. (Proverbs 29:27)

to Wise: _____

LIE: A pretty face makes for a pretty heart. (Proverbs 27:19)

to Wise: _____

LIE: Wealth lasts forever and we can take it with us after we die, so we should spend our lives chasing after it. (Proverbs 27:4)

to Wise: _____

LIE: Learning to control our actions is foolish. If it feels good, do it! (Proverbs 29:11)

to Wise: _____

Proverbs 28

Proverbs 28:13

People who cover over their sins will not prosper. But if they confess and forsake them, they will receive mercy.

Proverbs 28:14

Blessed are those who have a tender conscience, but the stubborn are headed for serious trouble.

DON'T COVER UP YOUR SINS!

When I was about five years old, I stole something. My mom stopped by the drugstore to pick up some things and while she was shopping, I asked if I could go look at the toys on the toy aisle. "Go look, but we can't buy anything today," she said as I raced off. For what seemed like hours (it was probably more like five minutes!), I paced the toy aisle making a mental list of all the toys I would buy if I had a million dollars. I was looking at one toy in particular when I heard my mother calling my name and telling me it was time to go. It was one of those plastic parachutes that is attached to a little army man that you throw in the air and the parachute opens up and the little army man slowly floats down. I really wanted to try it outside to see if it worked, and without thinking I grabbed it, put it in my pants pocket, and raced to the checkout to meet my mom.

I remember on the ride home feeling very guilty, but still I didn't say anything. When we finally pulled into the garage, my mom told me I could play outside for a few minutes until dinner. Finally! I had my chance to see if the parachute would really work. I took it out of my pocket and slowly unwound the rubber band that secured the parachute. Once it was ready, I climbed up in my tree house and dropped it down. And what do you know? It worked! It really worked! About that time my mom walked outside and saw me just as I was dropping it from the tree house. *"Where did you get that?,"* she asked. Uh-oh, busted. *"Uhhhh,"* I stuttered, *"at the drugstore."* She gave me a suspicious look and said, *"I don't remember paying for it at the checkout. How did you get it?"* At this point the floodgates burst and the tears started flowing. *"I promise, I didn't mean to steal it!,"* I cried.

My mom handled it pretty well and told me to get in the car. She headed right back to the drugstore and told me that I had to tell the store manager that I had taken the toy without paying for it. I was so scared in the car ride on the way over. Finally we were pulling into a parking spot and it was time to face my fear. She went with me and assured me that I would feel much better once I told the truth. I had folded the parachute back up as neatly as I could and wrapped the rubber band back around it to hold it tightly in place. My mom asked to speak to the manager while I held it tightly in my hand while staring down at the ground. I was so ashamed. When the manager finally approached and asked, *"How can I help you?"* the tears began to flow again. I handed him the parachute toy and told him through my tears that I had taken it without paying for it but that I was really sorry. He was super nice about the whole thing and told

me that while stealing was very wrong, he was proud that I had decided to do the right thing and return it.

Of course I wish I had listened to my conscience when I was on my way home. I knew it was wrong and I wanted to tell my mother to turn around so I could take it back. But I didn't. And you know what? As fun as it was to try the parachute out and see it float down from the tree house, I didn't really enjoy it much after the first try, because I knew that deep down inside it wasn't really *mine* to enjoy. Once I had finally confessed my sin and returned the toy, I felt a huge sense of relief sweep over me.

LISTEN TO YOUR CONSCIENCE!

JUST BETWEEN US

1. When I confessed my sin, who gave me mercy?

2. If I had been stubborn and chosen not to tell the truth when my mother asked me where I got the toy, how might it have led to me being "headed for serious trouble" in the future? (Proverbs 28:14).

3. Have you ever attempted to "cover your sin"? If yes, describe the circumstances.

4. Did you end up confessing it to anyone? If not, do you wish you had done so? (It's never too late!)

PSSST, GOD!

Pray and ask God to give you a tender conscience when it comes to sin. Pray that your tender conscience will keep you from committing a sin when you are tempted. If necessary, go ahead and confess to Him right now if there is something that is on your conscience that you need to share. He's listening and ready to give you mercy.

IN THIS CORNER
HUMILITY vs PRIDE

Every time you see the word *humble* in the Bible, it is talking about acting with humility. Everything about being a Christian is connected to the idea of humility—from loving God to loving others. So, what is it exactly? Simply put, *humility* is having a correct understanding of your true worth (or value) in Christ, and not in yourself. It means not having too high an opinion of yourself (or thinking you're "all that") and being aware that God is responsible for all the good things He does through you. Basically, *humility* is giving God the credit for all the good things about you and in your life. At the same time *humility* also means not having too low an opinion of yourself and understanding that through Him, we are priceless treasures!

Humility puts others' needs above our own. Jesus Christ was the perfect (literally!) example when He went to the cross and died for our sins. Not only that, but He served those around Him while He was on Earth by healing them, listening to their problems, and even washing their feet! Talk about humility! The perfect, holy, God of the Universe came to love and serve sinful humans! Whoa! That is, in a word, *humility*!

On the next page, rate yourself on a scale of 1 to 10 based on how you typically act. The closer to 1 you circle, the closer you typically behave to the sentence on the left and vice versa.

TEAM VIRTUE

VS

TEAM VICE

STAR PLAYER: HUMILITY

STAR PLAYER: PRIDE

Understands that your way is not always the best way.	1 2 3 4 5 6 7 8 9 10	Thinks that your way is the only way.
Thinks of others as better than yourself.	1 2 3 4 5 6 7 8 9 10	Think you are better than most people.
Asks for forgiveness when you do something wrong.	1 2 3 4 5 6 7 8 9 10	Usually only says sorry when someone tells you to.
When you make a good grade, you thank God for the blessing.	1 2 3 4 5 6 7 8 9 10	If you make a good grade, you tend to think, "I deserved that."
Gladly gives up a Saturday to serve others.	1 2 3 4 5 6 7 8 9 10	Doesn't really want to give up a Saturday to help others.
Lets others say the answers in class, even if you know them.	1 2 3 4 5 6 7 8 9 10	Always have to prove that you know the answers.
Graciously accepts feedback when others point out areas in which to improve.	1 2 3 4 5 6 7 8 9 10	Is easily offended when people point out areas in which to improve.
Thanks God for athletic ability when doing well in sports.	1 2 3 4 5 6 7 8 9 10	Knows that you're "all that" when excelling in sports.
Wants to please God more than people.	1 2 3 4 5 6 7 8 9 10	Is more concerned with pleasing people than God.
Look for the part you may have had in situations of conflict (fights, disagreements).	1 2 3 4 5 6 7 8 9 10	Immediately gets defensive and points out faults of others.

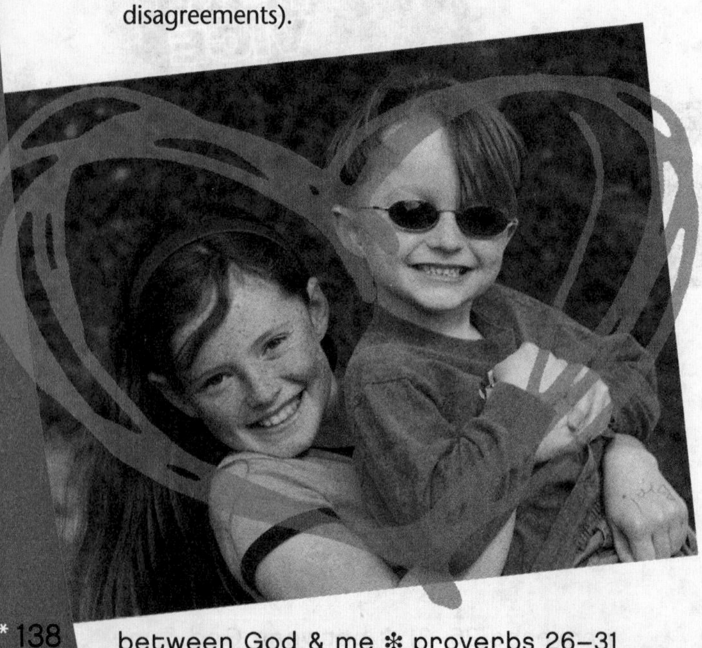

Now, total up the numbers you circled to see what corner you're in! How did you do?

KNOCKOUT!

If you scored between 10 and 39, you seek to live in a way that gives God credit. You strive to serve others and recognize that all your talent and ability comes from God. While you tend to make these wise choices, don't assume you always will. It is incredibly easy to slip into making prideful choices. Pray, pray, pray!

DANCING AROUND THE RING

If you scored between 40 and 70, you are in good company with most other people!
Like everyone, you sometimes give into pride. But, the good news is that you are at least trying to make the right choices! You know the right ways to live, but sometimes have a hard time living them out. Developing humility is something that will be a life-long process. What you can do, however, is practice changing your heart in some of the areas where you scored the highest. Pray first, and ask God for the strength and ability to choose humility over pride. It is definitely NOT easy, and certainly not our nature, so it will take some divine doing! When you begin to see improvement, remember to give God the credit and praise Him for helping you to look more like Jesus.

DOWN FOR THE COUNT!

If you scored between 71 and 100, you are having a really hard time in choosing humility over pride.
Pray and ask God to show you the "yuck" in your heart when you act prideful. Begin by taking three of the above statements where you scored an eight, nine or ten, and when those situations come up, pray for God to help you choose humility instead of pride. Be warned! When you pray for something like that, He usually answers in unexpected ways and gives you MANY opportunities to practice!

Proverbs 29

Proverbs 29:20 There is more hope for a fool than for someone who speaks without thinking.

Did I just say that???

If there was ever someone who has to work overtime when it comes to thinking carefully before she speaks, it's me. Using my mouth more than my brain has gotten me into a whole lot of trouble over the years . . . and occasionally still does. You would think I would have learned my lesson a few years ago when I got an invitation to a big party that one of my friends was throwing for another friend. I was so excited because all my good friends were going to be there. The day before the party I was trading e-mails with the birthday girl and I signed off with something like, *"Hey, I'll see you tomorrow night. I can't wait!"* Only one little problem: It was a SURPRISE PARTY and my friend had no idea some of her friends had planned it in her honor!

My big clue that it was a surprise party came when my friend replied back and said, *"Am I supposed to see you tomorrow night?"* Oh boy. I wanted to crawl under a rock and stay there forever. Or at least until the party was over. It ended up being okay because I told her that a few of us were taking her out to dinner for her birthday, so she was still surprised when we brought her back to a house full of people after dinner. But yikes, close call!

And then there was another time when I asked a woman at my church that I didn't know very well, *"When is your baby due, again?"* It seemed like she had been pregnant forever and wearing maternity clothes for at least a year. She replied and said, *"I had my baby about a month ago. Still trying to lose this baby weight, but it's coming off slowly."* Where is that rock that I can crawl under again? Please, someone put duct tape over my mouth before I embarrass myself any further!

Oh no!!

You probably have a story or two like mine where you said something that got you into trouble. It happens to everyone. We all make mistakes from time to time, but some people make a habit of speaking too quickly and making the same mistake over and over again. Proverbs 29:20 reminds us that, *"There is more hope for a fool than for someone who speaks without thinking."* While it's not always a bad thing to speak up and say what you're feeling, there are times when it isn't appropriate. I'm learning to pause and think before I speak, so I don't risk looking like a fool. And if someone as old as me can learn that habit, you can too!

JUST BETWEEN US

1. Can you think of a time where you spoke too quickly and found yourself in an embarrassing situation? If so, describe the situation.

2. How did you respond when you discovered your mistake?

3. If you are being honest, would you say that you have a habit of speaking too quickly and finding yourself in embarrassing situations?
Circle one: Yes   No   Maybe

4. If you circled "Yes" or "Maybe" above, are you willing to ask God to help you change?

Pssst, GOD!

Pray and ask God to help you learn to think before you speak. When you make mistakes, apologize to the person and move on. Those who check in with the Lord on a regular basis and ask Him for strength and wisdom, won't play the part of the constant fool.

Quiz

R U a wise guy (gal!)?

Follow this flow chart to see where you stack up when it comes to making some of the wise choices we have learned about in our study in Proverbs. Consider this your final exam! What did you learn from studying Proverbs? Let's find out!

You are invited to go to X with a group of girls at your school who aren't really known for their good behavior. You . . .

Decide to call some other friends to hang out that share your same values.

Your school is collecting clothing for victims of a hurricane who lost everything. You . . .

Go anyway because you know that this will make you more popular at school.

Don't really have clothes in your closet you want to part with, so you don't give anything.

As you're hanging out with these girls, they begin to talk about Stacy, a somewhat awkward girl in your class. You . . .

Stand up for Stacy and say something nice. They keep on gossiping, so, you realize this isn't the type of crowd to hang around with full-time. You call Mom to come pick you up.

Your school project is due on Monday and you are given an opportunity to go away for the week-end with a friend. You haven't started the project yet. You . . .

Agree with them, and add your own two cents. You're totally "in" with them now!

You're 30 minutes late coming home from hanging out with your friend who lives down the street. Mom asks where you've been. You . . .

Tell Mom you lost track of time and you are very sorry.

Lie to Mom and tell her there was an emergency, so you won't get grounded.

When your teacher praises the class for the number of clothes donated, you . . .

Gladly donate some of your clothes, including a few of your favorite shirts.

Smile, realize how blessed you are and look forward to other opportunities to bless others!

Proverbs-Committed
You are wise as an owl! You have learned about making wise choices when it comes to friend groups. You have also learned generosity and humility and your actions back it up. You see the benefit that comes from studying God's Word and let Proverbs really sink in! Don't get lazy, though. Be diligent and keep up the good work. Diligence, after all, is a wise virtue!

Brag to your classmates that you personally donated x number of items.

Proverbs-Confused
You've made some progress in this journey through Proverbs, but you still struggle with giving into gossip, following through with doing the right thing, and pride. You see the importance of learning, but seem to be having a hard time putting that knowledge into practice. *Wisdom* means applying the knowledge you have learned, so find the areas where you need some help and keep working on them! You can do it!

Admit to your mom that you haven't started the project and won't be able to go out of town.

Tell your mom that you've already done most of it because you really want to go with your friend.

Proverbs-Challenged
You showed up for the journey, but I'm not sure you let anything sink in when it comes to the wise virtues we explored in our journey through Proverbs. Start by listening to this advice (remember, wisdom does NOT ignore instruction): pray for God to open your heart to His wisdom. Then, start this study over again and put Post-its on the pages that talk about areas where you know you need to improve. It's not easy to practice making wise decisions, but it's worth it in the end!

Proverbs 30

Proverbs 30:24 There are four things on earth that are small but unusually wise:

Proverbs 30:25 Ants—they aren't strong, but they store up food for the winter.

Proverbs 30:26 Rock badgers—they aren't powerful, but they make their homes among the rocky cliffs.

Proverbs 30:27 Locusts—they have no king, but they march like an army in ranks.

Proverbs 30:28 Lizards—they are easy to catch, but they are found even in kings' palaces.

I've written before about Scout, my little 3 1/2 pound wonder-pup in a previous issue of Between.

I shared the story of how the little guy jumped off the top of the sofa when he was a puppy and broke both front legs. After eight weeks of hobbling around with two leg casts, I'm happy to say that he's back to jumping and running at rocket speed. You would sure think that he would be a little wiser after the sofa stunt, but I'm afraid not. He keeps our family in stitches with some of his clueless habits. Here's a small sampling of some of the not-so-smart habits he entertains us with on a regular basis.

1. When we go on a walk, he runs up to big dogs in the neighborhood and stands as tall as he can on his hind legs and bats them in the face trying to get them to play. Most of the big labs just stare back in confusion wondering where the little rodent came from.

2. If we accidentally leave the door to the pantry open, he jumps up on the bottom shelf and takes a flying leap into the garbage pail to dig for food. Only problem: He's too little to get back out so we usually walk in and see his little head peeking out the top . . . with some kind of food on his whiskers.

3. He has an obsession with chewing up writing pens. Even when we leave them up high on the kitchen table, he will jump up onto the chair, then onto the table, grab the pen, jump back down onto the chair, and then onto the floor and make his get-away to a hiding place where he can chew the pen up into tiny pieces.

And last but not least, he has a habit that leaves us all scratching our heads in confusion.

Let me warn you in advance that it's pretty gross. You might want to wait to read this one if you're about to sit down to eat dinner! At night, we keep both our Yorkies in a room downstairs in a small gated area with two doggie beds. For some unknown reason, Scout likes to drag small dried-up poopy turds into his bed and sleep with them. (I warned you it was gross!) Maybe it's to keep Lexie out of his bed, but seriously, couldn't he just sleep with a squeak toy or favorite stuffed animal?!

I think you get the picture. Scout, though small and adorably cute, is not real bright. However, Proverbs 30 mentions four things who are also small (like Scout), but unusually wise (unlike Scout!). Just as we can learn a lesson from watching Scout on what is not wise (especially that last one!), we can also gain a little wisdom from watching the four things that God mentions above. Maybe, I'll try to talk to Scout about those four critters and read him the verses!

JUST BETWEEN US

1. Read verse 25 above. What lesson can we learn from the ants? (*Hint: What can people learn about hard work from the ants?*)

2. Read verse 26 above. What lesson can we learn from the rock badgers? (*Hint: Does being "powerful" make you wise?*)

3. Read verse 27 above. What lesson can we learn from the locusts? (*Hint: If they have no king to lead them, how do they know to march in ranks?*)

4. Read verse 28 above. What lesson can we learn from the lizards? (*Hint: Do you think God gets a kick out of using lizards to remind powerful and wealthy people that even if they have the best security systems set up around their houses or palaces, they can't outsmart the lizard?*)

PSSST, GOD!

Pray and ask God to help you slow down and notice the world around you. Thank Him for the many things He has created that can teach us life lessons along the way.

P31 WORD SCRAMBLE

Unscramble these characteristics of the woman/wife described in Proverbs 31. Write each unscrambled word in the blanks and uncover what this woman does to receive praise!

Hint: look at these verses in Proverbs 31 for a clue

iinidfedg ___ ___ ___ ___ ___ ___ ___   ___ ___ ___   25

opereibsnsl ___ ___ ___ ___ ___ ___ ___ ___ ___ ___ ___   22

bhspitaleo ___ ___ ___ ___ ___ ___ ___ ___ ___   ___ ___ ___   20

(this is a tough one!)

dhar oewkrr ___ ___ ___ ___   ___ ___ ___ ___ ___ ___   13

ewsi ___ ___ ___ ___   26

gnsrto ___ ___ ___ ___ ___ ___   17, 25

hsalug ___ ___ ___ ___ ___ ___   25

theaesc ___ ___ ___ ___ ___ ___ ___   26

hnesusilf ___ ___ ___ ___ ___ ___ ___ ___ ___   16

dlveo ___ ___ ___ ___ ___   28

cimfleur ___ ___ ___ ___ ___ ___ ___ ___   20

espvidro ___ ___ ___ ___ ___ ___ ___ ___   15

What does this woman do to receive praise?

● ● ● ● ●   ● ● ● ●   ● ● ● ● !

Read the article about Proverbs 9 on page 42 for more insight about what this means!

Answers: dignified, responsible, hospitable, hard worker, wise, strong, laughs, teaches, unselfish, loved, merciful, provides

Proverbs 31

Proverbs 31:10 Who can find a virtuous and capable wife? She is worth more than precious rubies.

Proverbs 31:17 She is energetic and strong, a hard worker.

Proverbs 31:18 She watches for bargains; her lights burn late into the night.

Proverbs 31:20 She extends a helping hand to the poor and opens her arms to the needy.

Proverbs 31:25 She is clothed with strength and dignity, and she laughs with no fear of the future.

Proverbs 31:26 When she speaks, her words are wise, and kindness is the rule when she gives instructions.

Proverbs 31:30 Charm is deceptive, and beauty does not last; but a woman who fears the LORD will be greatly praised.

You may not have had the word *virtuous* on your list of spelling words yet, but if you had grown up a hundred years ago, chances are you would know exactly what the word meant. In fact, teenage girls from a century ago often wrote in their diaries about their desire to become "virtuous" women. Proverbs 31 is a passage that is known by many women of all ages. It gives a list of qualities that make up a virtuous woman. Back in Bible times mothers would often help their sons memorize verses 10–31, so they would know what qualities to look for when looking for a virtuous wife someday.

Today *virtuous* is not a word you hear mentioned much anymore. But that doesn't mean that it's not still important to become virtuous. So what does it mean? If you look *virtuous* up in the dictionary, you might find words like "good," "moral," and "pure." Those can be hard words to live up to, which is why Proverbs 31:10 tells us that a virtuous wife is "worth more than precious rubies." If you find a virtuous woman, she is like a rare and priceless gem or a sparkling jewel. It's one of the most important Bible passages for a girl to know.

Let's see if you can match up the following verses that describe a virtuous woman with words that mean the opposite (draw a line to connect them).

Verse 17   **Bad attitude; frowns more than smiles**

Verse 18   **Selfish, thinks of herself before others**

Verse 20   **Cares more about having a pretty face than a pretty heart**

Verse 25   **Lazy, rushes to get things done or doesn't do them at all**

Verse 26   **Wastes her money; quick to buy things she doesn't need**

Verse 30   **Speaks without thinking; rude and mean-spirited**

My favorite verse in the Proverbs 31 passage is verse 30 because it contains the most important quality of a virtuous woman: A woman "who fears the LORD." This basically means a woman who loves Jesus more than anything or anyone else in the entire world. She lives to please God more than people. If you can aim to live up to that verse, the qualities that are listed in the other verses will most likely follow. Girls who love Jesus more than anything usually care about the poor, work hard, speak with wisdom and kindness, and spend their money wisely. So, what do you say? Do you want to grow up to become the kind of woman who is like a rare and priceless jewel? Becoming a virtuous woman is worth the hard work and effort. The first step on your list: Fall madly in love with Jesus!

between God & me ✳ proverbs 26–31

1. Can you think of someone you know who is a "virtuous woman"? If so, who is it?

2. Even though we don't hear much about being "virtuous" in today's world, do you think it's still important to God?

   Yes   No   Maybe

3. Reread verse 30 again. What do you think it means when it says, "Charm is deceptive and beauty does not last"?

4. Do you think most women spend more energy and time on being beautiful on the outside or beautiful on the inside? Which one do you think God cares more about?

PsssT, GOD!

Pray and ask God to help you commit today to becoming a virtuous young woman. If you are weak in some of the verses, ask Him to help you improve.